Getting Started

an induction guide for newly qualified teachers

Henry Liebling

Published by Network Educational Press Ltd.
PO Box 635
Stafford
ST16 1BF

First Published 1999
Reprinted 2001
© Henry Liebling 1999

ISBN 1 85539 054 X

Henry Liebling asserts the moral right to be
identified as the author of this work.

Every effort has been made to contact copyright holders
and the Publishers apologise for any omissions, which
they will be pleased to rectify at the earliest opportunity.

Series Editor – Tim Brighouse
Edited by Carol Etherington
Cover design and layout by
Neil Hawkins of Devine Design
Internal layout by Val Kinsler, 100% Proof
Cover and internal illustrations by Annabel Spenceley

Printed in Great Britain by
MPG Books Ltd., Bodmin, Cornwall.

Foreword

A teacher's task is much more ambitious than it used to be and demands a focus on the subtleties of teaching and learning and on the emerging knowledge of school improvement.

This is what this series is about.

Teaching can be a very lonely activity. The time honoured practice of a single teacher working alone in the classroom is still the norm; yet to operate alone is, in the end, to become isolated and impoverished. This series addresses two issues – the need to focus on practical and useful ideas connected with teaching and learning and the wish thereby to provide some sort of an antidote to the loneliness of the long distance teacher who is daily berated by an anxious society.

Teachers flourish best when, in key stage teams or departments (or more rarely whole schools), their talk is predominantly about teaching and learning and where, unconnected with appraisal, they are privileged to observe each other teach, to plan and review their work together, and to practise the habit of learning from each other new teaching techniques. But how does this stage of affairs arise? Is it to do with the way staffrooms are physically organised so that the walls bear testimony to interesting articles and in the corner there is a dedicated computer tuned to 'conferences' about SEN, school improvement, the teaching of English etc., and whether, in consequence, the teacher leaning over the shoulder of the enthusiastic IT colleague sees the promise of interesting practice elsewhere? Has the primary school cracked it when it organises successive staff meetings in different classrooms and invites the 'host' teacher to start the meeting with a 15 minute exposition of their classroom organisation and management? Or is it the same staff sharing, on a rota basis, a slot on successive staff meeting agenda when each in turn reviews a new book they have used with their class? And what of the whole school which now uses 'active' and 'passive' concerts of carefully chosen music as part of their accelerated learning techniques?

It is of course well understood that even excellent teachers feel threatened when first they are observed. Hence the epidemic of trauma associated with OFSTED. The constant observation of the teacher in training seems like that of the learner driver. Once you have passed your test and can drive unaccompanied, you do. You often make lots of mistakes and sometimes get into bad habits. Woe betide, however, the back seat driver who tells you so. In the same way, the new teacher quickly loses the habit of observing others and being observed. So how do we get a confident, mutual observation debate going? One school I know found a simple and therefore brilliant solution. The Head of the History Department asked that a young colleague plan lessons for her – the Head of Department – to teach. This lesson she then taught, and was observed by the young colleague. There was subsequent discussion, in which the young teacher asked,

> *"Why did you divert the question and answer session I had planned?"*

and was answered by,

> *"Because I could see that I needed to arrest the attention of the group by the window with some 'hands-on' role play, etc."*

This lasted an hour and led to a once-a-term repeat discussion which, in the end, was adopted by the whole school. The whole school subsequently changed the pattern of its meetings to consolidate extended debate about teaching and learning. The two teachers claimed that, because one planned and the other taught, both were implicated but neither alone was responsible or felt 'got at'.

So there are practices which are both practical and more likely to make teaching a rewarding and successful activity. They can, as it were, increase the likelihood of a teacher surprising the pupils into understanding or doing something they did not think they could do rather than simply entertaining them or worse still occupying them. There are ways of helping teachers judge the best method of getting pupil expectation just ahead of self-esteem.

This series focuses on straightforward interventions which individual schools and teachers use to make life more rewarding for themselves and those they teach. Teachers deserve nothing less, for they are the architects of tomorrow's society, and society's ambition for what they achieve increases as each year passes.

Professor Tim Brighouse

Contents

Acknowledgements

So many people have either directly or indirectly helped to make this book what it is. The errors and omissions are all my own work. I have tried to acknowledge all references to the work of others.

Thank you to:
Jim Houghton at Network Educational Press for his enthusiasm and flexibility;
Carol Etherington, the editor, for making the book more coherent and readable;
Emma Crocker for her comments, work on sources, resources, web sites, restructuring and proofreading;
Francesca, my youngest daughter, for such honest, thorough, precise and clear guidance and comment on reading a very rough first draft;
Cynthia, my wife, for her encouragement, patience and advice whilst I struggled with this my first book;
Peter, my brother, for the many discussions comparing induction into medicine and induction into teaching;
My past colleagues, some of whom are referred to in the book;
Current colleagues, especially Paul Spurgeon for the original inspiration, Tony Brown for his wisdom and permission to use some of our joint writing (See Chapter 5), Joanna Haynes for notes and guidance, Wendy Clements and Ann Clarke for help in deciphering some of my jottings, and Jim Christophers for his help in reconnecting me to secondary practice;
So many children, pupils, students, teachers, lecturers and advisors, but especially David Acres, Nick Appleby, Emma Binney, Carol Breakwell, Howard Davies, Demelza Elliot, Lindsey Fear, Rob Green, Sue Pybus, Chris West and Kate Whitehead;
Jean-Philippe Maquaire for his good humour and keeping me electronically intact and in touch.

This book is dedicated to Hans, my late father, a polymath, my best teacher and guide, and to Molly, my grand-daughter, who is letting me share in her excitement and wonder as she discovers the world around her.

Henry Liebling
October 1999

Introduction

At the beginning of my induction year, I felt as if I'd been thrown in at the deep end. I had to deal with my class and also be the art co-ordinator. But the induction programme really helped me.

Primary NQT

Major influences on what should appear in this book stem from my own views and experiences as a very naughty attention-seeking child, confused adolescent, doting father of four daughters and, I hope, a caring teacher. I have learned much from children's and young adults' views since 1968 and teachers' and student teachers' views over the last 14 years.

What makes a 'good teacher'?

Asking ex-students and new teachers this question on my INSET courses has proved invaluable. Their honesty and blunders make me realise what I painfully remember myself; that is how hard the transition is from student to teacher and often how lonely and misunderstood you can be. Partners who don't understand, colleagues and heads who tell you that you are coping really well when you feel that you're not, unanswered questions and answers to problems you didn't yet know existed, all feature. My favourite piece of unhelpful advice is "Well, I thought it best to just let you get on with it!" This is like learning to swim by being thrown off the high diving-board into the deep end. What I have attempted to do in this book is to search out a range of strategies and ideas in the hope that you will find some of them useful in the transition from student to teacher. I hope that, as you feel more confident, you might use some of the strategies to help the children and young adults that you teach to become better at coping themselves and learning how to learn. I have only scratched the surface in trying to introduce most of the ideas and hope that if you are interested you will follow up the references.

I'd like you to use this book to help you to develop your self-confidence and self-esteem as a teacher. Use the chronology of The First Year (See Chapter 1) to help you through the induction process. Pick out the bits that might support your needs. If you are still interested at the end of the year or want to find out more, then use the references, especially the web sites.

You have the absolute right to ignore, invert or subvert any of the rules, suggestions, or guidance offered in this book if it helps you to become a better teacher! Follow your heart. If it doesn't feel right; then don't do it. From time to time, I may seem to offer directly conflicting bits of advice. This is because:

- We are all different, in some cases very different.

- We react differently in different situations and with and in different groups of people.

- My current understanding of the way the brain develops and works leads me to believe that we might need to treat different parts of the brain differently in order to 'get through'.

To provide the best quality education for their pupils, schools need teachers who:

- work with each other, classroom assistants and other non-teaching staff and talk about their teaching;

- work, study and research together in a sustained, meaningful and positive manner;

- work with tutors in HE to disseminate and share their results from both primary and secondary phases;

- widen their repertoire of teaching methods and evaluate their effectiveness;

- observe one another, not to assess their teaching, but to share good practice in order to improve the quality of children's learning.

Good teachers also need to consider how they will deal with a range of the following dilemmas:

● A teacher must cope with about 30 children.	➔ The majority of useful exchanges occur between a teacher and no more than four children.
● In order to operate, we need a degree of uniformity.	➔ We want to encourage diversity of activity, response and experience.
● We recognise that concrete materials benefit most young children.	➔ We want to encourage children to think about abstractions.
● We want children to discover things for themselves.	➔ We want them to come to some common conclusions.
● We want to know what we are trying to do.	➔ We want to encourage exploration of new situations.
● We learn from experience.	➔ This can lead to stereotyped actions.

● We want to give children the security which comes from repetition.	➔ We want children to be able to deal with insecurity.
● We need to make some plans for children in advance.	➔ We don't know our children until we have met them.
● No textbook is satisfactory.	➔ We cannot make up everything from our own resources.
● We cannot tell in advance the effect of anything we ask children to do.	➔ We have to act on the assumption that we do.
● No teacher wants a syllabus.	➔ Every teacher wants a syllabus.
● Mathematics gains its present place in school through its usefulness to society.	➔ Mathematics earns its present place in children's experience through its enrichment of that experience.
● We want children to understand what they are doing.	➔ We do many things fluently precisely by NOT thinking about how they work.
● The range of mathematical activities in which children can engage is infinite.	➔ Children have only a finite amount of time in school.
● We want to know the best way of doing things.	➔ Often, there is no best way.
● We aim to build up confidence in children.	➔ We are lacking in confidence in ourselves.
● Children should be treated as individuals.	➔ Children need the stimulus of other people for their intellectual growth.

From Notes on Mathematics for Children, *ATM, 1985*

Developing your teaching

You might not realise just how much your values and beliefs influence what you really care about in your life. This in turn influences your views about teaching, learning, pupil behaviour, the role of the teacher and the purpose of education. Look at the pros and cons of teaching: the laughter and the tears. Plan your career in teaching: where will you be in five years' time? Use your intuition to get the right first job for yourself: does the place feel right? It is more important to get good support during your first few years than more money or higher kudos. Decide when to move on or quit, if it isn't for you. Two or three years in one place might be long enough. Teaching is a 'right livelihood'. Think about your role models and those teachers who have inspired you. Develop and stick with your vision of education.

Looking at the theories

Most of the ideas in this book can be found elsewhere. However, I am still working on the notion that there may be a parallel between each of the three great psychological theories of learning this century: Behaviourism, Constructivism and Social Constructivism and the three parts of the brain described by MacLean: the Reptilian, Mammalian and Primate brains. The interaction of the Limbic system with the Reptilian brain may account for much of Behaviourism, focusing as it does on stimulus and

---

response. The development, firing up and sequencing of the three parts and numerous modules of the brain may go a long way to explain Constructivism, with its emphasis on the developing organism interacting with its environment. The integration of the three parts and the resonance between that level of integration as the individual develops and other knowledgeable mediating individuals accords with Social Constructivism. If I am right, even in part, then this may go some way to unravelling the mystery of teaching and learning.

Since the early part of this century, with the advent of nuclear particle physics, a new paradigm has emerged: holistic, systemic, non-determinist, and we are witnessing the death throes of the old one: reductionist, determinist and Descartian. I'm sure that there are significant links between teaching as an activity and complexity theory. We have hardly begun to apply the latest neuroscience research to mainstream education. Isn't it about time we did? (See Chapter 7 for more on this.)

Teaching is a complex personal activity. We need to be risk takers, not neutral technocrats. Aim to start some action research as soon as possible. Look up any of the ideas I've mentioned that appeal to you. You need to see yourself as a policy maker rather than a policy complainer (See Pollard A.,1997, Chapters 14 and 15 for guidance on taking action). You are involved in how education is conducted and improved. If you are a primary teacher, you are one of the first cohorts to emerge trained to implement the National Literacy Strategy (NLS) and the National Numeracy Strategy (NNS) and satisfy the standards for qualified teacher status. This includes the requirements for subject knowledge in the core subjects, ICT and your specialist subject if it is a foundation subject. If you are a secondary teacher, you are likely to take on the role of form tutor and pastoral duties as well as your input to your subject across the school.

As you work through your induction year, with all of its demands on your time, remember to respect children's integrity; expect them to do amazing things. There is a great need for diversity in education and in the workplace. Children can learn much without formal teaching; make sure that you make a difference.

Part 1: Organising your teaching

Chapter 1

THE FIRST YEAR

"Be yourself: we liked you when we hired you!"

Headteacher

Chapter contents:

- **Between appointment and taking up your post**

- **An overview of the induction year**

- **Induction into the school and into the profession**

Between appointment and taking up your post

There are some key ways in which you can prepare yourself to start your new post.

Observing and teaching before you actually start

You will find it really helpful if you can observe teaching during the term before you start. This might be a class you will teach, a teacher you will work with or your induction tutor. It may be that your school requested that you teach before the interview so that they have already seen you teach. All of these should help you to feel that you can fit into the new school and work in a way that suits both you and the school.

Getting hold of the school's paperwork

This can include the school's mission statement, brochure, policies, plans, schemes of work, and specific texts or resources that you need to familiarise yourself with, e.g. software. There has been no shortage of paper to take home and work on. I suggest you use a number of highlighter pens and 'post-its' to mark what you need. Transfer specific bits of information either into your notebook or diary. OFSTED inspectors have to base their judgements on evidence and some of this is paper-based. They are looking for resonance between what is on paper (intention) and what they observe (practice). Schools now have policies and statements on every aspect of the school's life and function. There are also many nationally produced statistics and documents, many available free and most on the Internet. You should find the School Development Plan useful, as well as the actual plans for the curriculum. The following should be invaluable:

- the staff handbook;

- an induction handbook;

- department handbooks (secondary) or subject curriculum documents (primary);

- the school development plan;

- schemes of work;

- lists of resources;

- pupil records;

- the school's prospectus;

- a staff list with responsibilities, rooms and telephone numbers;

- a plan of your classroom(s) and a plan of the school; a local OS map might also prove very useful;

- your timetable if it is available, or a copy of the current one if it will not change too much;

- a calendar for the next academic year which details the key events.

I still advocate, produce and use a year planner onto which I put all the important dates. How else can I be proactive and avoid getting caught out? I still find it imperative to put all the information which is relevant to me into an A5 diary using my own code. I can then predict and plan for difficult periods in the year when the workload is likely to be higher and so avoid taking on too much during that period. You might choose another method. Make sure your electronic personal organiser hasn't got loose batteries like a friend of mine's. It fell on the floor and the batteries fell out. He lost all his data. Luckily, we could recover the information from my detailed planning documents. He's back to pen and paper!

Try to discuss this volume of paper with your induction tutor. They will be able to lead you through it and help you to prioritise each document; highlighter pens and post-its at the ready! (See Chapter 3 for further guidance on Time Management.)

Determining priorities

One way to sort out what you need is to use your Career Entry Profile (CEP) as a source of your strengths and needs. If you can discuss this with the headteacher or another senior member of staff before you take up your post, then do so. Your strengths should help the school to place you in the best situation for both them and you. You need to become aware of and accept that the school has needs and priorities; which they will match to some of your strengths. Look at the school development plan and read the most recent OFSTED report, or ask about the main points in both of these. Ideally, your appointment will contribute to satisfying some of their needs and priorities. Also, the school will have a staff development plan which you need to be part of. Don't be afraid to offer to help with areas of school life that you are interested or experienced in, but be wary of taking on too much in your first year. Saying yes is easy, saying no is much harder, and getting out of a promise is best avoided.

Getting to know your induction tutor

Your induction tutor is likely to be the most important person to you in your new post, so the quality of your relationship is fundamental. Try to find out something about them, such as interests that you might have in common, but particularly what they really believe in and care about in education. What makes them tick as a teacher?

Over the years, I've had all types of mentors. The first was a strict disciplinarian who loved his subject and wanted to impart his enthusiasm to young and old alike. Another fancied himself, dressed as the big white hunter and had grandiose plans, but he was kind and gentle with me and eventually I even managed to carry through some of his high expectations. A third I'll always remember for her love and sense of humour. We often laughed with or at the wonderful things children do or say. She was always there when I needed her. She never panicked and always had a kind word for everyone. The children knew that she cared and so did I. More recently, I'll never forget a colleague's honesty, integrity, patience, good manners and dedication to his students, willing them on to achieve their potential.

The point I'm making is that each had something to offer. I needed to find out what it was and match it to my needs at the time. Each one has left a mark. Here are some of the things I learned from them:

- Be firm and consistent.

- Have high expectations and believe in the people you work with. By believing in them, you help them to believe in themselves.

- Behave well yourself. Try to set a good example; you are a role model.

- Work with love and humour, not taking yourself too seriously in this transient world.

- Know why you wish to spend your life as a teacher. You will have to defend it.

- Encourage and support your pupils.

- Make time to say 'Please' and 'Thank you' properly to all those you work with, both above and below you; it really matters.

- Celebrate achievements; your own as well as those of others.

Finding out about your class(es)

The current class teacher or subject teachers can give you much valuable information about the pupils you will be teaching next term. Ask for a thumbnail sketch of each child if you can. Try to get access to their records and learn about particular problems or issues that you should know about. I still look for dissonance between standardised test scores if these exist. For example, what would you make of a child who does very well in non-verbal reasoning or art or design, but is below average in English and average in mathematics? Ask yourself what is going on here.

I am still very interested in how people are progressing and if they know about it. Many are unaware of how well or badly they are doing. Some have great strengths and others great needs that sometimes they are unaware of. Make it your business to find out and try to negotiate with each learner what are their strengths and needs. Then you can help all of them to draw on and develop their strengths and encourage them to work on their needs.

Another way to find out about the children you will teach is to watch them in class and in the playground. Then talk to them and to their teachers about what you have noticed. You will never be in such a dispassionate situation with them again.

An overview of the induction year

What might the first year be like?

It is useful to outline what many believe to be the main three phases of a typical induction year. It may well not feel typical to you, but remember that many have passed this way before. You may well pass through these phases more quickly or more slowly, but don't worry; it is not a race.

Term 1
Phase 1
Asking for help; The first few days; The first few weeks; Getting comfortable with your preferred teaching styles
Phase 2
Starting to improve teaching and learning; Developing a successful environment for learning and teaching
Term 2
Phase 2 continued
Further improving teaching and learning; Maintaining a successful environment for learning and teaching
Term 3
Phase 3
Extending your teaching repertoire; Moving out of the classroom

Phase 1

Asking for help

Do not be afraid to ask for help. Ask whom to ask. If you have followed my advice earlier in this chapter, then you will know who is responsible for what. See how long it takes you to put names to faces.

In my experience, school secretaries, caretakers, classroom assistants and technicians have proved to be an excellent source of help, insider information and wise words. They are worthy allies and deserving of your respect. They have usually seen it all before; including curriculum change, and teachers coming and going.

The first few days

Get to know the children if you didn't get the chance during the summer. Use some of the techniques suggested in Chapter 2. Look at Chapter 3, especially the section on time management. Plan for transitions; make sure you know about registers, dinner registers and timings for assemblies, breaks and so on.

Look at Chapter 3, which also deals with organising the classroom, and Chapter 4 on managing behaviour in your new school.

The first few weeks

Make sure that you plan to be seen teaching and to see others teach and talk about what happens. Go through the Standards and pick out those that you can easily work on at the start of the year (See Appendix A). Discuss these targets with your induction tutor and pencil in the date for the first formal meeting. You should have three across the year. Try to be clear about when and what these meetings are about. You don't want surprises later. Aim for three further meetings across the year to discuss issues relevant to your development. This should then work out at one meeting every half term or six weeks.

Getting comfortable with your preferred teaching styles

Concentrate on feeling at ease with the material and the teaching style. You will then start to notice the children more and your own performance less (See Chapter 2). Use your evaluations, the children's work and their views during plenary sessions to confirm that you are doing a reasonable job (See Chapter 5). Try to track significant achievement. Do not be dismayed if you feel tired, rushed and do not feel that you are teaching as well as you did on your final teaching practice. Try to work SMARTER rather than harder (See Chapter 3 for advice on time management and stress management). Be kinder to yourself. Talk to your induction tutor about how you feel. Are you getting to know the children well enough so that you can tell where the problems are? Are you trying out some of the ideas for transitions and break states (See Chapter 2)?

Phase 2

Starting to improve teaching and learning

Look again at the Introduction, then read Chapter 6 on Models of Teaching and Chapter 7 on The Appliance of Neuroscience. Start to consider whether you could build some of these ideas into your teaching, and if you could use your understanding of how pupils learn to improve the quality of their learning.

Developing a successful environment for learning and teaching

If you didn't get the chance earlier, you should now take stock of the classroom environment and, having worked in it for a few weeks, make up your mind about how things could be changed to improve your teaching and pupils' learning. Look at the section in Chapter 3 on organising the classroom.

Further improving teaching and learning

Try to measure success by how much progress your pupils are making (See Chapter 5). Learning can take place in many different ways and not always just how we predict it (See Chapter 8). Use the section on noting significant events in Chapter 3 and relate this to the advice on action research in Chapter 9, to help you to unravel problematic issues in your teaching or the pupils' learning.

Maintaining a successful environment for learning and teaching

Continue to review your practice against the advice on classroom organisation in Chapters 3 and 8. As your teaching styles develop, do you need to reorganise your classroom to reflect any changes?

Phase 3

Extending your teaching repertoire

Look at your Career Entry Profile again. How well have you managed to use your strengths and satisfy your needs? Read Chapter 9 on understanding ourselves and others. Use your assessments and records (See Chapter 5) to determine where to focus your attention. If you have been working on significant events, then what areas need exploring further? Re-read Chapters 6 and 7, looking for supportive suggestions. If you have been working on one area and wish to deepen it, is there a web site that might help? When you are being assessed against the QTS standards and, more especially, the induction standards, use the Traffic Lights (See Appendix A) and Standards Support (See Appendix B) to be found at the end of this book.

Moving out of the classroom

Look for further opportunities to extend the range of your teaching environment by the use of artefacts, visitors, the school grounds, and visits and field trips to museums, galleries, historic buildings, civic facilities and environmental sites in the local area.

The Appeals Procedure

Hopefully, you will not need to worry about this as you will have completed your induction year successfully. However, if you fail or are given an extended induction period, read the procedure carefully and make an appeal. The consequences are too serious not to. You can always withdraw your appeal. Be prepared to sacrifice your Summer holidays for your future.

Induction into the school and into the profession

You need to realise that there are two significant but different aspects to your induction: induction into the school and induction into the profession. The new national induction system is designed to give some sort of parity to induction into the profession, by having a specific set of induction standards. LEA or other advisors will offer support, but this is likely to vary across the country. Your union will also wish to help you in the transition to becoming a teacher. The new General Teaching Council will have a role to play in your professional life. Induction into the school is more like joining a huge family, and entails getting to grips with the highly individual nature and organisation of each school. You liked the school when you accepted the job and they must have liked you as they offered you the job.

Finding and devising support systems within the school

Your most important support systems are your induction tutor, the headteacher and other members of staff in the school and, locally, the LEA and your fellow cohort of NQTs. How much use you make of these support systems is largely up to you. If you are proactive and organise regular meetings for local NQTs and make contact with old friends and tutors, you can extend the size and scope of your personal safety net.

Making good use of your Career Entry Profile

I normally suggest that my students complete their CEP strengths and needs with their new headteacher in mind. You know what you have achieved during your course and what strengths you will bring to your first post. Discuss your strengths and needs with your headteacher, head of department and induction tutor. Ask about the school's needs and targets. See where and how you might be able to match your needs and targets with those of the school. Look for common ground; remember that your strengths meet their needs, which is hopefully why they appointed you in the first place. Sometimes, your needs match their needs so there is likely to be INSET or some other training provision made. If you have looked at your school's most recent OFSTED inspection report, then you will be aware of the school's identified needs. The school development plan is another place to look for common ground. What has been done recently and who was involved?

Try to offer strength in curriculum areas where you have qualifications or experience or both, such as your main subject or an interest you have pursued for a number of years. This will help the school to fit you into the existing structures. You might, for example, offer English and RE based on your areas of study and academic qualifications, but offer music and outdoor education because of your personal interests. Do not ignore your personal interests. They can strengthen your potential both during lessons and extra-curricular activities. I have always believed that your enthusiasm is one of the most important things that you bring to your teaching. For example, I have seen children inspired by teachers who loved dancing yet held no formal qualification in it.

Some features of successful induction schemes

The new induction arrangements for England are built on previous experience both here and in many other countries which have also struggled to implement and maintain successful induction programmes for their teachers, helping them bridge the gap between 'student of teaching' and 'teacher of students'. All over the world, newly qualified teachers feel overwhelmed by the challenge of their first year in charge of a class. Beginning teaching doesn't appear to be any easier in other countries and few governments, if any, are satisfied with even the best programmes. Here are some of the features of the best induction programmes from around the world. Nearly all of them have been built into your new induction programme:

New teachers are viewed and valued as professionals embarking on a continuum of experience and responsibility. Beginner or novice teachers are not expected to fulfil the same demands as experienced teachers. This might take the form of a lighter teaching load or not being given the most challenging classes in the school during your first year. The school must ensure that you do not get a full teaching timetable. The guidelines recommend a 90% teaching load over your first year. This could be 10% release per week or time taken in blocks. You should not expect to teach the more demanding classes in the school. Your first year is not meant to be a baptism of fire. It is expected that you will work hard and that your contribution to the school will grow as you are given appropriate support and encouragement. So it is most important that you act, behave and feel like a teacher from the start, even if you know that you will be assessed during the year. You are now a teacher and not a student.

In my first teaching post, a wiry rugby-playing Welsh CDT teacher, whom the pupils really looked up to, became my self-appointed mentor. All the classes were great, apart from one which I taught for three lessons per week, each as problematic as the nightmare class portrayed in a popular TV programme of the time, or so it seemed to me. Without the support, positive caring attitude to his pupils, dry humour and encouragement of this colleague, I wouldn't have lasted a term.

New teachers are looked after, nurtured and encouraged to interact with other teachers as much as possible, by:

- the provision of an induction tutor;

- working closely with another teacher;

- watching one another teach at least once per week;

- asking for and being given advice;

- a good variety of interactions with other staff;

- making time for planning and feedback from observations;

- regular evaluation sessions, which set targets for improvement.

Your headteacher might decide to be your induction tutor or appoint another teacher to take on this important role. You might find yourself in the class next to an experienced teacher who would be only too happy to help you and answer your questions. This teacher might be your induction tutor. Both of you should feel free to wander in and out of one another's classrooms as you work together, watch one another teach and ask for advice. You must not allow yourself to become isolated from the other teachers in the school.

A good variety of interactions with other teachers, such as team teaching, curriculum development, planning meetings, staff meetings and regular meetings with your induction tutor will help you to feel part of the school and contribute to the organisation, planning, assessment and evaluation procedures in use. You will need some dedicated time for planning together, either with your induction tutor or the other teachers in your year group or planning team. Hopefully, you will be involved in planning for the whole school or one key stage in at least one curriculum area, which you will have identified as a strength.

You will also need time to observe your tutor and other teachers teaching and for you to be observed teaching on a regular basis, for example once per week, and to discuss this and get regular feedback on how you are doing. You might be able to organise observation of other teachers in other schools, including exchanging observations with another NQT. You should get regular evaluation sessions so that you know where you are going, by setting targets for improvement with your induction tutor at least once per term; though perhaps half-termly would be better.

The emphasis is on new teachers getting better through support and encouragement rather than on assessment of teaching standards. Frequent observations of and by the new teacher makes the assessment process less threatening. Assessment is seen as formative rather than summative. In England, it may be hard to play down the role of assessment in the induction year, but it is essential that the induction tutor's support doesn't revolve solely around the standards for passing the year, just as it would be foolish to ignore the standards.

The induction process is valued and has a real purpose for both the tutor and the new teacher. You must ask for help when you need it. Make a list of questions and issues. Keep asking questions. Do not act apologetically about this, as we all need to learn. Do you get cross with learner drivers? Should you? Try asking for help from a number of members of staff, not just your tutor. Identify and match your strengths and needs to particular members of staff. Ask if you can help with a club or particular area of interest. Explain to a curriculum co-ordinator that you have needs or expertise in their area and note carefully their response. Be sensitive to and become aware of individual responsibilities, workloads and internal politics.

In my first primary teaching post it was a wonderful, unflappable, funny and kind class teacher who freely and willingly shared her considerable expertise and resources with me, whenever I asked for help. I could only do 'real writing' and the six-year-olds could not read it. In one ten-minute coffee break, she taught me a printing script suitable for infants, then she helped me plan appropriate work for six and seven-year-olds because I had been used to teenagers and adults.

The school should have a culture of shared responsibility and support in which nearly all the staff are involved in some way in making new members of staff feel welcome and help them to settle in. The best schools have a culture or even a mission statement which reflects this. The school is a learning environment for all who work there, adults as well as children. Personal and professional development are encouraged and supported. "Drink from a flowing stream rather than a stagnant pool."

In one school, which was new to me, where I'd been appointed head of maths and IT, I had a door between my classroom and that of the very experienced head of English. He often popped his head around the door to excitedly share children's work with me or answer my endless questions on the children, the staff, the routines and the running of the school, or to lend and borrow equipment, but he never made me feel ill at ease and his enthusiasm for his subject was infectious. He was so genuine that he really made a difference to my settling in.

The deputy head always had a knack of knowing what I'd need and apparently effortlessly supplied it. The whole staff pulled together and I have happy memories of performing science experiments on the staffroom table first thing in the morning. These teachers wanted to keep on learning and trying out new ideas. They wanted to share their thinking with one another, even if it meant an argument. They were equally as prepared to share their failures as their successes: "Why did that approach not work?", "What on earth happened?", "What could I have done instead?", "How could I have avoided that?", "How could I have improved the lesson?" They wanted to surprise the children into learning things that they didn't think they knew. They wanted to challenge them in all aspects of the curriculum, not just the core subjects.

Chapter 2

GETTING STARTED WITH YOUR CLASS

You've got to pace yourself. Don't try to do everything at once. Take time to get to know your class but remember to make time for yourself as well.

Secondary NQT

Chapter contents:

■ **Starting activities**

■ **Getting to know your pupils as individuals**

■ **Balancing pupils' demands with your ability to satisfy their needs**

■ **Getting to know yourself as a teacher**

Starting activities

Here is a collection of activities to get you started on working with your new class of children, pupils or young adults. You will need to adapt the activities to the age of your pupils. If necessary, seek advice on the suitability of these activities for your pupils. The activities are designed to help you and them work on:

● interpersonal intelligence, group dynamics, transitions in the classroom, sharing ideas and debate;

● intrapersonal intelligence, dialogue with self, coping with stress and anxiety, and visualisation.

I've classified and coded the activities as follows:

O   Needs you all in a circle. These could be part of circle time or form time.

+   Fosters and encourages self-esteem and a positive attitude to self and others.

A   Is quite active and will need space and possibly acting or role-play.

W   Results in a written record or artefact of some sort which could be kept.

R   Offers opportunities for reflection and review.

Starters and name games

Getting to know one another, learning to work together, and appreciating the strengths and needs of others is probably your best first course of action. Here are a few ideas. You only need one or two that you can use and adapt to break the ice. If the children know one another well, perhaps too well, then consider carefully which activities might be revealing for you as their teacher. Most of the activities are based on examples from Pike (1988) and ATM (1987).

Introduce yourself with a positive adjective. "I'm Happy Henry", "I'm Sympathetic Cynthia", "I'm Magical Molly". You might need lists of positive adjectives, collect them to start with or use a dictionary for a few minutes before starting the activity. [O +]

Say your full name and clap out the rhythm of the syllables. The group copies the rhythm. [O A]

Form pairs, preferably in a circle. Tell your partners about yourselves, then listen as they tell you about themselves. Now introduce one another to the rest of the group. This is good for a first meeting. I take notes and try to remember some feature or characteristic to help me remember their name, for example Jazzy James (plays jazz guitar), Serious Sarah (as opposed to Smiley Sarah) were three of my last year's postgraduates. Some people prefer to picture the person with something to do with their name. So a Jenny Smith might be remembered with a blacksmith's hammer and anvil. I prefer to link to a hobby or interest. [O +]

Say your name and throw a soft ball or rolled up cloth to someone else. Keep going and try to include everyone. Repeat alphabetically. [O + A]

Say the name of the person you are throwing to. Try not to miss anyone out. [O + A]

Make a label showing your hobbies or interests with your name in the middle and stick it to your clothes. You could get pupils to design a sampler. I had great fun with personal T-shirt designs on the theme of 'What would you like people to know about you?' [+ A W]

Activities for getting to know one another

Finding things in common: Everyone has or makes a list of the whole class. In pairs, try to find a common interest, skill, hope, like or dislike. Once found, write the item beside their name, discuss briefly and change partners. Get a set of 4, 6 or 10 or until the whole class have met up. [+ A W R]

Musical Meetings: When the music stops, shake hands with the nearest person; a different person each time. Exchange personal information. [+ A]

People Hunting: From a list of 20 attributes (e.g. plays an instrument, sings, runs, draws, sews, knits, looks after siblings or relatives, gardens, keeps pets or other animals, dances) or recent events (e.g. just had a special day, learned a new skill, visited another place, town, country or relative), write the name of anyone you can find who fits the attribute or has experienced the event. Discuss their feelings. Try to get at least one person for each of the 20 attributes or events; you could make it 10 or any number. [A + W R.]

People Recipes: Students describe their physical appearance and character in the style of recipe ingredients; method optional. For example, take a good length of medium brown hair, two appealing hazel eyes, one very inquisitive nose, a full cup of laughter (leave the giggles in); add a heaped soup spoon of mischief and a pinch of rascal. [+ W R]

Team-building activities

Friendly Tree: It could be based on any suitable topical object. Cards are stuck or hung on branches. Each card has a friendly act written on it. Each child or each group or one child or one group select a card to carry out that day, for example talk to someone you don't often talk to; help someone with their work; write or draw a friendly note; make someone smile. [+ W R]

House points, stars, stickers, certificates, merits, and tokens: The use of these depends very much what the exchange value is or if the recognition is enough. A letter home is very well perceived by children and parents. You could discuss rewards as a data-handling activity to decide democratically as a class or tutor group what rewards would be best. What type, style and design should we use for certificates and letters home? What should be exchanged for merits, stars or house points? [+ W R O]

I'm not so bad really: This was suggested by my eldest daughter when I was feeling particularly fed up. Collect and keep all the positive cards, thank you and appreciation notes which you receive as a teacher. Re-read them during dark times! For the pupils, get them to make a collection of certificates, positive statements, memories, and a family tree. This could lead to an autobiography for English or a portfolio. [+ W R]

Mime, action, expression and gesture: Sit in a circle. Perform an action such as 'brushing your teeth'. The next person repeats your action and then adds their own such as 'blowing your nose'. You or the next person or anyone in the group can say what they think the action is or they can stay silent and try to work it out. The next person repeats the first two actions and then adds theirs, such as a 'sneeze'. This is like "My granny went to market and she bought…", a good memory game. Help one another. Try to encourage good performances of the mimes and increasingly subtle use of gesture, facial expression or mime. Review performances, commenting on well chosen actions, unusual actions, and good strategies for remembering. They will enjoy this and get better and better at it if you persevere in the search for 'quality' [+ O R A]

Mime with precious, rare, delicate or dangerous object: Sit in a circle and mime passing an object to the next person. You could use a crumpled piece of paper, cloth, sponge or nothing. The group has to guess what object you are passing on. Is it a precious jewel, dying bird, beautiful rose, jelly, beetle, snake, small furry creature, hand grenade, sharp knife, dirty nappy, full glass of wine, or a hot cup of tea? [+ O R A]

Fortunately, unfortunately: Sit in a circle. One starts off with "Fortunately I was in time for school today." The next continues, "But unfortunately the teacher told me off for not bringing my homework." The next continues "Yes, but fortunately..." and so on. The story must make sense and, as with any circle game, a pause or mistake can lead to the person being eliminated, though I tend to make them non-competitive. [+ O]

There is more than one way: Split the class into six groups. Give each group the same message, which they must communicate to the whole class after about 30 minutes, using one of the following media (no real words, letters or numbers are allowed): musical instruments; modelling clay; mime using your bodies in silence; paint, crayons or felt pens and large sheets of paper; black and white paper with scissors and glue; speaking in a made up alien language using intonation and expression. The message is "Let us work together in friendship". The preparation time can be drastically reduced to five minutes if you select mime, music and alien speech. The discussion following such an activity may well reveal hidden talents and novel ways of responding to tasks in the future. Above all it should heighten your and their awareness about non-verbal communication potential and how they might become involved in planning their own work and way of responding. [+ A W R]

Puppets: Use socks with elastic bands, buttons, beads, sticky paper and re-enforcing rings to make hand puppets or draw faces on a paper bag. Make your own collection of puppets. Puppets are an excellent way to increase confidence, use of voice, expression of feelings and opportunities for acting, both for children and their teachers. I used to write on the blackboard with a glove puppet on my left hand over my right shoulder. The puppet was looking at the class. They would confide in the puppet and respond to questions put by me in the daft voice of the puppet. Children can learn to read and tell stories using puppets and make up their own scripts and scenarios for role-play. [A + R]

Break states: brain gym activities and other rhythmic patterns

Break states are just that: a way of breaking the current state to change activity, release tension, revitalise, relax, start or effect a smooth transition or ending. I've known teachers use a whistle, piano chords, march, play Simon Says, get children to mimic the teacher's stance and gestures, and play Chinese whispers. One wonderful infant teacher sings instructions to her children and they sing back. Here are a few ideas to get you started. Some of them are taken from Alistair Smith's *Accelerated Learning in the Classroom* (Network Educational Press, 1996). Use, modify, develop, collect, share and enjoy these activities.

Brain gym activities aim to connect the left and right sides of your brain. This should help to improve motor co-ordination. The activities can be used to manage transitions, sustain motivation, and to boost interest and energy levels. They are quick and effective ways to change the physical and mental state of your class at the start, during or at the end of a session.

Double Doodle: On cheap paper, using pens or large wax crayons or coloured chalk, draw large shapes first clockwise and then anti-clockwise. Then change hands. Then use both hands together. Try to produce the mirror image. I have found that balancing up clockwise and anti-clockwise movements really helps some children with their handwriting. Look out for those who can only go one way either clockwise or anti-clockwise. I'm sure it is related to handedness.

Skywriting: Use Double Doodle techniques in the air. This is cheaper, faster and non-threatening for pupils with special needs, and you can assess the whole class very quickly. Try letter formation, spelling words, numbers, formulae, shapes, in fact anything. Say the letter, word or idea as you move your hands. Try going larger and then smaller, slower then faster. Try using both hands but to create mirror images or to produce the same pattern with both index fingers tracing out characters in the same direction.

Cross Crawl: Stand up and march on the spot. Touch your raised knee with the opposite elbow. You can try this lying on your back. Try the Austrian version (no need to wear the Lederhosen!): touch your left heel with your right hand behind your back, then the right heel with the left hand.

Crossed Hands: Cross your hands in front of you. Turn your palms to face one another. Put hands together and interlock your fingers. Bring thumb down, towards chest and up past your nose. Now get a partner to point at one of your fingers without touching it. Try to move that finger. Try again and swap roles. Not so easy is it?

Rub-a-Dub: Yes, this is the one where you have to try to rub your tummy whilst patting your head. Change hands. Change actions. Change the rules. This is good for taking your mind off something.

Alphabet Edit: Use the alphabet or any series of numbers, letters, words or symbols that you want to learn, written on an OHT or sheet of paper or on the board. Try the alphabet, prime numbers, the periodic table or reactivity series. Under each letter, word or symbol put *L* (put up your left hand), *R* (put up your right hand) or *B* (put up both hands). Say the letter, number, word or symbol as you do the movement. Start slowly enough to cope, then speed up as you get better. This is much harder than it looks, but strangely restful and invigorating. Try the example below:

A	B	C	D	E	F	G	H	I	J	K	L	M	N	O	P	Q	R	S	T	U	V	W	X	Y	Z
L	*L*	*R*	*L*	*R*	*B*	*R*	*L*	*B*	*B*	*L*	*L*	*R*	*L*	*R*	*B*	*R*	*L*	*B*	*L*	*R*	*R*	*R*	*L*	*B*	*L*

H	He	Li	Be	B	C	N	O	F	(elements in periodic table)
L	*L*	*R*	*L*	*R*	*B*	*R*	*L*	*B*	

Fizz, Buzz: Choose two numbers, e.g. 3 and 5. For every multiple of 3, the group must say Fizz and for every multiple of 5, Buzz. You then start to count around the group from one, putting Fizz, Buzz or Fizz Buzz when necessary. A mistake results in elimination. Some people include any number with a 3 or 5 in it, such as 13 or 51. 51 is 3 ˇ 17 so must be Fizz but could be Fizz, Buzz. [O + R]

Visualising: This can be numbers on a number line or working on geometry in the mind. Close your eyes. Imagine a blank panorama. Give it a background colour. In the distance is a dot on the horizon. As it approaches, you can see that it is a square in a contrasting colour. It is getting bigger and bigger. Now it fills half of your view. Stop it, push it back to make it a reasonable size again. Try rotating it slowly one way and then the other. Let it settle and then stretch it until it makes a good rectangle. Roll it over onto its short side. Squash it back to a square again. Stick the base to the ground but pull the top side so that it becomes a rhombus. Stretch it into a parallelogram. Put in the diagonals. Return it to a square and let it disappear into the distance. Tape record the instructions to practise and get it right.

Evaluation, review and feedback activities

This is a huge and increasingly important area. National Numeracy and Literacy strategies have stressed the importance of reviewing the work done. For years, teachers have used a 'Show and Tell' at the end of a lesson or series of lessons. Accelerated learning techniques, especially 'Suggestopaedia', have worked on improving recall using music and reviewing the main concepts by reading them out quietly at the end of the lesson to a background of specially selected music. I offer you a few suggestions:

How are you feeling today? Use a set of pictures with facial expressions and a paperclip to show how you feel today. Try a mood chart similar to a weather chart. An ex-navy commander I knew used to wear his black gown in a style which reflected his mood and gave us fair warning of what to expect. Wrapped tightly around himself meant he was grumpy (a rare event); normally worn and all was well; off the shoulder, he was in a laid back mood; slung over his shoulder meant we were in for a treat, something special. I remember his kindness, sense of fun and fairness, but especially that huge grin when we responded with good work. He was captain of his ship and non-verbal communication was clear.

Speedy evaluations: How do you feel about the work that you have done this week, this morning or this lesson? 'Thumbs up' means positive; 'palm flat' means 'so-so'; 'thumbs down' means negative. Try a smile, plain face or grimace. How about a wave with both hands, one hand or not at all to signify how pleased you are about your progress? Add a Gallic shrug and covering your eyes with your hands. Ask everyone in turn to say something that they have learned. They can say "pass" if they wish. Keep a learning log and write down what you have learned and what you want to learn next. Get one or more groups to report back to the class on what they have been doing. Get one group at a time (one per day) to present the main points of the lesson back to the class. It is far too easy to run over and not leave enough time for evaluation, feedback and review.
Try to make hooks from one lesson to the next. Try to leave time for bridging (see Chapter 6).

Other short activities

Try silence. Use silence for children to write, if they wish, for just a few minutes. Perhaps give them a few minutes' silence to draw a response to some event. Use a few minutes' silence to encourage meditation or prayer. Develop intrapersonal skills; the dialogue with self without which you may never really come to know yourself.

Read a short poem (haiku), riddle (koan), short story (Zen story), a potted biography, a passage from Gilbran's *The Prophet*. Use respectfully any short passage of any scripture. I once used the Annunciation story from the Koran to good effect. Hindu scripture has some wonderful prayers, songs and stories. The parables are an obvious choice. I've also used many quotes from Spike Milligan, Oscar Wilde and Chief Seattle, to name a few. Let children have their own ideas; don't immediately try to explain or expound on the text. *Philosophy in the Classroom* M. Lipman et al., suggests many books with suitable stories and pictures.

Many of Edward De Bono's activities and ideas can be used in five or ten minutes. The National Numeracy Strategy videos show teachers using a series of short activities to start the maths session. In some cases, the pace and level of interaction and involvement is impressive. You could also encourage children to make quick mental maps and concept maps to record and work on ideas.

Endnote

Apart from the obvious benefits and uses of these types of activities, if you watch and listen carefully, you will quickly get to know about the children you work with. They blossom, unfold and reveal their true selves in some of these activities. You will see another side that is not normally elicited by schoolwork. The playfulness and risk-taking involved is not really optional for those who wish to thrive in the next millennium.

Getting to know your pupils as individuals

Another important way to get started is to watch and listen. Look out for:

- unusual behaviour or body language;
- unusual questions or speech;
- unusual work, written, drawn or made.

Ask the child's previous teacher about them, but don't be overwhelmed by this information. Use your own instinct; use and trust your insight; then look for evidence.

Check and sort out relatively simple things, such as can every child hear and see properly, or as well as they might be able to? You will be amazed at what you find. Eyesight can change dramatically around puberty. Hearing can change with the seasons.

Talk to your induction tutor and the SENCO about particular concerns such as:

- children who shine in some areas and subjects but not others (help them develop and expand on their strengths);
- children who prefer to respond in only one mode or not at all (drawn, written, spoken, acted out);

- children who seem incapable of following a set of instructions (try and encourage them more or make the instruction set smaller);

- those whose demeanour and behaviour are worst after the weekend, half term and holidays, or children who appear depressed (this is not uncommon, but it is rarely recognised and seldom accepted);

- children who can do all the work but say they are bored all the time (how can they be challenged?);

- those who have a particular highly developed sense, such as hearing or smell (they may well comment on or over react to sounds or smells);

- children who knock things over, leave a trail of destruction, or bump into other children (they might be 'clumsy');

- children who take you completely literally and struggle to communicate (they could have Asperger syndrome or be Autistic).

In short, get to know your pupils and help them to get to know you.

If you look at lists of recommendations for able children, very young children, those that are struggling, EAL and so on, you will find common features of good practice, reflected in the ideas below:

- Have sound rising expectations and tell them they can achieve these targets and expectations. (These should not be too high, too low or rising too fast: can't cope, or failing; all of these extinguish any enthusiasm.)

- Based on what they feel they need, make verbal or written contracts with pupils. "I promise you that by the end of the year, your spelling will have improved, so long as you do what I ask." (You might want a shorter time and more specific target.)

- Agree on SMART targets and negotiate tasks with pupils. (Try a 'wish wall', where children write on a card what they are 'stuck on' or want to learn about.)

- Have interesting, challenging tasks to work on. Ensure that some required strategies are in place beforehand, e.g. group work, presentation, discussion, opening up problems and investigations, and activities for getting started.

- Involve your pupils in the planning. Using Highscope (See Chapter 7 and the Bibliography), four-year-olds plan, do and review, so why not you and your class?

- Give positive encouragement and intervention. Give and ask for feedback and value their work. Make your praise specific.

- Use and expect a wide range of responses, resources, sources of information and support. See Gardner's Eight Intelligences (Chapter 8) and Forms of Communication (Chapter 7).

- Ask questions and ask for questions.

Balancing pupils' demands with your ability to satisfy their needs

Think about how you organise the limited time available for dealing with pupils' needs. Look at those times when pupils might need your input:

Are you the limiting factor in your classroom?

How can you encourage children to take more responsibility for themselves and their learning? Have you made rules for use of rubbers, broken pencils, sharpeners, dictionaries, getting words, going to the toilet, getting paper... Should you? Ask them.

Do you have sensible procedures for any or all of these? Do the children know? Do they understand why?

Transitions and changing tasks

This is often the high-risk time when things go wrong. Can you phase the changeover or get it done quickly and efficiently? Some teachers use an egg-timer, traffic lights, keeping a record of the time taken to get changed for PE and seeing if the record can be broken, or counting to ten!

Demanding help and re-explanation

Here are some ways of dealing with pupils who demand your attention:

- ask three before you ask me;
- one minute to settle and silence for the next five minutes;
- limited queues: no more than three each side of me;
- going around the groups: the bus route. Remember to have your 'bus depot stop' where you rest and take stock of the whole class, scanning each child.

Marking policy

Must you mark all of their work? Can they mark their own and one another's maths? Should they become aware of their mistakes and the mistakes of others, or should you be responsible for finding all their mistakes? "Do you know where you went wrong?" "Do you know why?" "Can you sort it out yourself?" "If you get stuck, come back and I'll help you." Provide answers if possible. Encourage self-help and peer-help. Respond to children's work constructively and positively, dealing with some specific aspect of the work, probably agreed beforehand. Why are you marking their work?

Recording tasks

Should children keep a record of their own work? Some teachers put up the tasks for the day or even the tasks for the week and then leave it to the children to plan what they will do and when they will do it. They might mark it off on their list once it is completed and the teacher has seen it.

Starting with questions

Consider the questions that you want to ask about the topic. "What have you found out?" "Can you answer your own or someone else's questions?" Could the class plan their own topic? Could they gather resources for the topic? Could they devise a set of tasks, which can be added to, for themselves? Some teachers encourage each child to have a folder with the tasks listed and ticked when they are started and highlighted once completed. For a book-based topic, such tasks might include:

> design an alternative book cover; write a character description of one or more of the characters; write a synopsis of the story or one chapter; write about what happened before the story starts; write a different version of Chapter 2; write a different ending; produce a crossword for the book or topic; a word search; make a data file on characters or relevant objects; make up a cross-number puzzle; devise a quiz for the topic.

What shall I do next?

Pupils need not necessarily come to you when they have finished. Provide meaningful activities which children can get on with without demanding your attention or special resources, for example interactive displays of science toys, magnets, mirrors or artefacts. List activities which they could move onto, such as reading to one another, reading plays, improvising, recording, scripting, resourcing, producing and performing their plays.

Rewards and praise

Devise a range of strategies to use when individual pupils, small groups or the whole class have done well. These could include:

- a letter home;
- extra break time;
- special games, a quiz or hangman;
- marbles in a jar to earn a treat;
- taking work to show it to another member of staff or the headteacher.

Getting to know yourself as a teacher

Returning to school as a teacher

As an NQT, you are required to act, perform and behave as a teacher, yet you may well feel as if you are the 'little one' again, especially walking into a busy school staff room. Should I knock? Where can I sit? Do I need a cup or mug of my own? You may be forced to relive old nightmares from your school days. Worse still, a colleague may remind you of an adult with whom you had, or still have, a problematic relationship. You must be honest with yourself about how you feel and what you are thinking. In many cases, you will be able to laugh it off, and see the funny side of being on the other side now as a teacher not a pupil. If not, then talk to someone about it as soon as possible; get help.

Falling into the trap of regressing to be a pupil

Whilst you must consider the children's wellbeing alongside your own health and sanity, you must at all costs avoid appearing to side with the children against the staff. If on your return to full time school as an NQT you actually feel more like a pupil than a teacher, it is very tempting to act like one. It might even be fun for a while and make you feel less ill at ease, but it is a potentially fatal strategy for your acceptance and further professional development. So accept your feelings with honesty and talk to someone you trust as soon as possible.

Building on strengths

It is highly likely that they the way you teach is influenced by two major factors:

- how you were taught;
- how you learn.

Think about how much you have learned in your life without any formal teaching. Now think about what you were formally taught, by whom and how. Which teaching methods worked well for you? Which do you feel didn't help you to learn effectively? I'm a great believer in finding out what people are good at and helping them to develop that first. This will give you much needed self-confidence, show you in a good light to pupils and staff and help you build a secure base to your teaching.

However, you need to be aware of those areas where you don't feel confident. Perhaps a cutting remark, a feeling of confusion, sense of pain or failure at some point in your life stopped you from developing music or physics or gymnastics or mathematics. As you remember that event now as an adult, do not be surprised if the original emotions are still present. We remember these events with the values and beliefs which we held when we were that age, or with the raw emotions of a pre-verbal toddler. To break down these barriers is very hard. Our brains are designed for survival and we need to remember dangerous or threatening events, so that we can avoid them if we meet them again. Unfortunately, our original reasons, seen through the eyes of a five or six-year-old, or a sensitive 14-year-old, might be seriously flawed. Perhaps we should have taken no notice of the laughter at our attempts to sing, of a page of our neatest work scrawled across in red ink or the lack of insight into a dark painting done at a time of sadness. But we did and, sadly, we still do, feel the anguish.

Being sensitive to children's needs and fears

As teachers, we must be sensitive to those we work with. Some people are easily put off learning anything new. Failure breeds failure just as success breeds success. If I were to ask you what you are not very good at as a teacher and then force you to do it in front of others, how would you feel? Some children may believe every word you say, every smile, every gesture and every frown. A chance careless remark or cruel jibe could destroy trust between you and a child, which has taken time and patience to build.

Encouraging others to try again and supporting their efforts

If we can overcome these feelings of failure, perhaps we ought to try the task again. We might not be brilliant at it but we'll probably cope, undoubtedly improve in time and hopefully feel empowered as a result. "I never thought I'd ever be able to draw, swim, do maths," or whatever. It brings me the greatest joy as a teacher to support pupils, then watch them doing it on their own. Like learning to ride a bike, suddenly the realisation comes that the 'scaffold' has been removed and they can do it on their own. Life is hard enough as it is. Remember that you don't have to do it all on your own. In fact, we need to support one another at all stages in our lives.

Can we do this for those we teach? As Tim Brighouse says "Can we surprise them into doing something they thought they couldn't do?" Ask children what they'd like to be able to do and help them achieve it. Ask yourself what you'd like to be able to do and look for help and guidance.

Chapter 3

ORGANISING YOURSELF

In the first few weeks, I was concerned that I wasn't really getting to grips with any real teaching. But my induction tutor said that it is normal to feel like this and I should concentrate on getting classroom routines in place and control established.

NQT

Chapter contents:

■ **Time management**

■ **Making important decisions**

■ **Noting significant events**

■ **Stress management**

■ **Organising your classroom**

Time management

We all have to learn to cope with too much to do and not enough time to do it in. Here are some useful strategies to consider:

- Learn to say 'NO', or 'perhaps', or 'I'd rather not'. Give choices.

- Try to handle each piece of paper only once. Get a bin or a big box. Recycle the paper and feel good about putting paper in the bin. OR pass it on, delegate, pass the buck. OR deal with it and put a post-it on it to remind you what you've decided to do with it. OR try using two piles: 'today' and 'sometime this week'. Re-sort the second pile every weekend. OR put it in the pile of forgotten papers in a temporary 'throw away' box. Bin everything when the box is full!

- Don't respond to notes and memos with more notes and memos. Go and talk to people face to face. What do they really want? Sort it out in one go and perhaps make a friend. In a big school, or if you need it in writing, a memo is sometimes necessary. Try e-mail for groups of people you need to notify.

- Use e-mail if you can and you like it. It is quick and easy. You can deal with it when you want to. It can form a good record. It is often terse but chatty; and is therefore good with people you know. You can save time, paper and stamps and even make new friends. E-mail a trusted university or college tutor to get advice or just keep in touch. They might be pleased to hear how you are getting on. E-mail me, I might be able to help or advise you {hliebling@marjon.ac.uk}.

- Form an e-mail group of NQTs with your colleagues, friends and/or other local NQTs.

- Keep a diary large enough to hold the daily information you need. Number the weeks of all the terms. Put in dates as much ahead of time as you can, for example parents' evenings, INSET days, external examination dates and departmental meetings. Some people prefer a wall calendar, used in the same way. Put in all holidays, half terms and Bank Holidays and plan to do something positive with your own time. Plan to go away for the weekend, or visit friends or relatives. There won't be any 'my time' unless you plan to make it happen. Calmly, firmly and quietly explain that you are not available on certain evenings. You don't have to say why. Yoga, sport, a pub quiz, sailing; these things take absolute priority if you wish to remain sane and survive. Don't weaken! (Hot tip: find out when any of the SMT members have fixed weekly evening activities, and plan your social life on that night. I guarantee it won't be over-booked or trampled on!)

- Don't leave it until it is urgent! Plan ahead. Try to distinguish between those jobs that are urgent and those jobs that are important (who says so?). Ask the school secretary's advice whom to ask about what is deemed urgent and important or discuss things with your induction tutor.

	Urgent	Not urgent
Important	Take deep breath and deal with it. Could this have been avoided? Who should have dealt with it? Who could deal with it next time?	Make time to sort it out properly. I can't deal with this now. See me … Make an appointment. Put it in your diary. Make time.
Not important	Is it really not important? Take 10 seconds to deal with it or ignore. It might be really important to a child. Do it now?	Deal with it as, when and if you want to. Don't use it as a distraction to avoid more important work. Might it become important?

- I make priority lists. If I can deal with something quickly and this will save me time later, then I get it done. If it is important, then it deserves your whole-hearted attention and time to do the job properly. All too often, we have to deal with other people's urgencies that are not urgent or important to us. Why, for example, should you answer the phone in the middle of a scheduled appointment or meeting? The chances are somebody else's 'urgent' is about to trample on an agreed 'important'.

- Teach specific ideas, tell the pupils what these are, set related specific homework, mark specifically, for example don't mark every mistake, only those you and the pupils are targeting or focusing on at the time, such as punctuation, spelling, layout, structure, novelty, development, audience, accuracy, graphics or humour. I've used Victor Borge's 'Phonetic Punctuation' for years to make it clear that I was on the look out for good punctuation during a specific period of a few weeks or days.

- Use computers for pro formas, lesson plans, timetables and standard letters; in fact anything you are likely to re-use and probably modify. Simple spreadsheets can really help in keeping track of marks and grades. Remember that you will need to register under the Data Protection Act if you keep records on your computer. You may be able to use the school's system. Keep security copies, and file them safely.

- Part of the time problem is that you are having to do so many things for the first time. Next year it will be easier, especially if you can find this year's version. I always put the year in my file names. There is a discipline for eight character file names. *Windows95* or later lets you off the hook, but you still need to make them sensible and memorable. Start a new folder with directory tree and disk each year:

Year group, e.g. 2B, 3X. They then all get listed together.	List (LST),register (REG), course outline (CO), plans (PLN).	Letter (LET), book list (BKS), subject, e.g. maths (MA).	Year starting Sept 2001 is (2001) all year, or use months. Use a version letter, 01a.

- Directory structure and your filing system are important. Is everything at one level or buried ten levels deep? Is everything in the same file marked miscellaneous or general at one extreme, with hundreds of files each with one item in at the other? Get help! Keeping old material separate and similar content together reduces problems and eases finding files.

- Future, current, archive (i.e. old but I might need to refer to them again!) is one system which I use. With colleagues working on the same course material, we e-mail one another with new versions, put them on a secure network and use a 'shuttle' disk. I tend to keep word processing, spreadsheet, graphics and music on different disks. I still don't trust computers, especially networks. Keep backup copies in a safe place. Do not begrudge the cost of a new disk to archive your work. Move to ZIP drives or burn your own CDs soon!

- Coloured A4 envelope files (or colour-coded wallets) fit in tidy boxes and filing cabinets and are handy, cheap, and easy to write on and identify. Some teachers prefer ring files.

- Large A3 paper, pencil and rubber is still often much better than using a computer for complex plans and work in progress. I often use computer-generated planners, but work on paper copies with coloured pens and a pencil, which I type up when I'm ready. Try using wallpaper offcuts to develop ideas on. Post-its are great for collecting ideas, shuffling and prioritising; for example today's jobs with the most important and urgent at the top. Take pleasure from crossing one off. Any more is a bonus! If you end up with fewer jobs on your list at the end of each day than you started with, then you are winning. If not, then delegate, say no, bin them, desert or resign!

- Even the longest journey begins with just one step. Getting started on a daunting task is often the hardest part. Start with something easy or that you enjoy doing. Don't keep putting it off. Carve up big tasks into manageable chunks. Set aside a sensible amount of time to do each chunk. Make the job fit the time. If you finish sooner, you can do a bit more, start something else or stop. Do what you can in the time. Perfectionists take care! It is easy to be conscientious and rob yourself of rest, sleep and leisure. A balanced life-style is not a luxury; it is essential to your well-being. There will always be more that you could do, and never enough hours in the day. Balance and diversity will help you to become a more effective teacher. Be kind to yourself.

- When marking, try to comment on the understanding of the concept in question, the range or type of strategies used and the personal qualities or attitudes displayed by the work. This will help you to give specific, positive and constructive feedback. Offer a next step wherever possible.

- Manage your teaching day. Look at the pattern of each day. Make a plan for the day. How active or passive will you be, and will pupils be, across the day? Look for the transitions. How will you cope with these transitions? (See Chapter 2 for break state activities.) The change in intensity of energy that you expend across the year, term, week, day, lesson, session and each classroom activity has a rhythm; the pattern is fractal in nature. Which lessons and topics are more demanding of your preparation time and need more of your energy to sustain them? Try to allocate activities between those that are more demanding for you and those that are less demanding.

Making important decisions

"Just because we can, it doesn't mean we should." Lillian Katz

In your first year of teaching, you may have important decisions to make. Obviously, you will be able to ask other colleagues for advice, but it is a good idea to consider ways of approaching decision-making. Edward De Bono has suggested several:

- **CAF:** Consider All Factors. Generate lots of ideas, then select most appropriate ones to choose from. Committee folly results when committees take the first sensible suggestion and accept it, eager to get on and get through the agenda.

- **PMI:** Plus, Minus and Interesting. (See a summary in Fisher R., 1995.) Edward De Bono's PMI technique is very easy to use by making a grid like the one overleaf on a sheet of A4 paper:

Plus	Minus
Interesting	

- SWOT Analysis:

Strengths	Weaknesses
Opportunities	Threats

Divide a sheet of A4 paper into four. This is simplicity. Aim for effective, elegant, simple solutions (De Bono, 1998). You might be interested in other 'Advance Organisers', such as Pete Smee's Brain Box, Mappings, Mind Mapping and Concept Mapping. (See the list of web sites in the Bibliography for details.)

The six hat technique: This is an excellent way to check out all avenues, even if you are on your own. In a group, it gives people permission to operate in a variety of ways without being considered strange or out of character. You do not need to use all six hats every time, nor does everyone have to respond to them. However, it is useful to allow comment on a few of them in some defined order. Make sure you have exhausted one hat before you go on to the next.

Six thinking hats: a parallel thinking approach to meetings

White hat: (neutral)   INFORMATION (available, needed, missing, fact, rumour or opinion)

Red hat: (fire, warmth) FEELINGS (current intuition, emotion, hunches without any explanation)

Green hat: (new shoots) POSSIBILITIES (time and space for creative effort, search for alternatives, provocation, movement, new directions, speculation, vision, lateral thinking.)

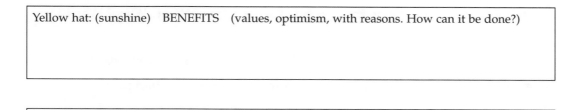

Yellow hat: (sunshine)   BENEFITS   (values, optimism, with reasons. How can it be done?)

Black hat: (judge)   CAUTION   (criticism, risk assessment, fit with values, policy, objectives...)

Blue hat: (blue sky, overview)   THINKING   (orchestrate thinking, facilitate procedures)

Use in any order. Work together. All wear the same colour hat; one colour at a time.

Noting significant events

A significant event is something that simply 'sticks in the mind'. Unlike many things that happen to us and which we struggle to remember, we have no difficulty in recalling where we were at the time, who we were with, what was said, and so on. Although some of the details may be lost later on, and the sense of immediacy may fade, nevertheless a significant event can remain vividly with us for a long time.

Writing about significant events soon after they occur helps to retain a sense of their vividness and complexity. Writing allows us to capture and explore their importance to us. A written note aids the process of reflection and increases the richness of our insights into our mental processes, our feelings and our belief systems. A further stage is to offer our writing to others for discussion and analysis, for example you might discuss some significant events with your induction tutor. The interest for your tutor, in what are significant events for you, lies in their need to stay in touch with what is important for you as a beginner teacher. Exploring significant events with peers is another powerful way in which we can gain deeper insights into ourselves as teachers.

We don't always know at the time that an event will remain memorable. When we realise it has some significance (even though we may not know yet what that is), then it's time to make a brief note. An event may cause us to see ourselves, and others, in a different way. Very often, a significant event carries with it a strong emotional charge. We may feel elated or angry, excited or depressed. We may be left with a sharpened perception or a memory stirred up from deep within us. We may feel we've gained a clearer sense of our own thinking, feeling or values. Some events present us with a dilemma; an embarrassing impasse, a feeling of being 'stuck'.

Getting started with a file

A significant event has to be important to us. It does not have to be significant for anyone else. When we have such an event on our mind, we need to go over it and write some notes. A few sentences are enough. A useful note will probably contain:

- brief factual information about people's actions: Who? What? When? Where? How?

- details of how we felt at that moment (we may not have those feelings later);

- brief speculations about what we think made the event significant;

- the date of the event and the date of writing.

Keeping such a file is designed to prevent you from writing about everything, and help you focus on really significant events.

Reviewing significant events

We need to be able to sort one event from another. Writing on cards allows us to sort and group the cards in different ways. Single cards can easily be shown to other people. The greatest insights to our teaching can come when cards are re-read some time after the initial writing. New insights often arise during the re-reading. These new insights can then be added to the card and the whole event re-examined. You will be able to track what has been of importance to you over the year.

Stress management

Only the mediocre are always at their best.
                                                    Graffiti

In coping with stress, anxiety and feelings of inadequacy, we can all remember with embarrassment daft or terrible things we have done. An ex-naval Chief Petty Officer I worked with some years ago asked me, when I sheepishly confessed to a dreadful 'cock-up', "Will they still be talking about it in 20 years time?" "Good heavens, no!" I replied. "Then what are you worrying about?" he said. I often remember his advice and relate it to others.

We care what others think of us. We don't like to let them down. We want to do a good job. All of that is fine, but not if it makes us ill with worry every time we make mistakes. There is a Yorkshire saying: "The man who never made a mistake never made owt."

Often, we are like rabbits trapped in the dazzle of on-coming headlights. My friend and colleague, David Acres, in his excellent book *How to pass exams without anxiety*, covers meeting coursework deadlines, organising revision, improving your memory, taking exams, coping with anxiety and using others as helpers. Some of this may be of direct use to you. Much of it may help your pupils, even if they aren't yet old enough to have exams!

Signs of stress

Here are some of the more obvious signs of stress:

- Are you smoking, drinking or eating more or less than usual? Comfort seeking?

- Are you more sensitive to the actions and comments of others? Tetchy?

- Are you having difficulty getting to sleep, or waking up earlier than normal?

- Do you feel you must work when others are playing or relaxing? Can you delegate?

- Are others aware that you are shutting yourself off and not really listening to them?

(Cook, 1992, in Bloomfield, 1997)

It's not the situation, it is how we respond to it that may cause the stress. Some people cope every day with potentially highly stressful situations such as hospital casualty staff, firemen, police, or ambulance drivers attending crashes or disasters. You need to know your limit. Be wary of becoming like Boxer in *Animal Farm*, always blaming yourself and believing that everything will be all right if only you work harder. It will only be better if you work SMARTER.

Different individual personalities are likely to respond differently to the same situation. A colleague once recommended and praised me as a good member of staff to take on school trips and school holidays by saying "Our Henry is good wi' sick". How would you cope? Would it worry you?

Avoiding stress by catching it early

- I like to give an overview, a map of where we are going, what Alistair Smith calls 'the big picture'. For many, this is a comfort and reassurance.

- Go over what you hope will happen. This relieves pupils' stress and yours.

- Deal with their worries sooner rather than later, then get on with your business.

- Take time out, have a break and make space for reflection. Learn and use Yoga, alternate nostril breathing, meditation or visualising.

- Try to rehearse or imagine the next bit. I often suggest 'videoing' your lesson in your mind and replaying it to see what is missing or likely to go wrong once you have planned it. Imagine the room you will be teaching in and where the resources are. Do the logistics work?

- Try to work more intelligently, more effectively; SMARTER rather than harder. Mark for a specific purpose rather than for everything. Encourage pupils to mark their own work. Involve colleagues and pupils in planning. Share your problems. Give colleagues and pupils choices rather than always feeling you must do everything. If you want me to do A, then I'll have to drop or reduce either B or C. Give senior staff choices; show that you have thought about the problem. Recycle as much as you sensibly can (very hard when you're just starting!). Senior managers actually normally suffer less stress than their juniors do if they are in control. Are you a tough personality or a one-ulcer person in a two-ulcer job?

> It's not like any of my teaching practices. I am in charge of it all
> and there are so many things to juggle.   NQT

- SMART targets are better for you are your pupils. The are stated positively and they are:

Specific   **M**easurable   **A**greed   **R**ealistic   **T**ime-based

- Look at SWOT analysis and other decision-making devices mentioned earlier in this chapter. You need 'creative mediation' of that which is thrust upon you. Believe you have the power to transform it. Give yourself permission to control it. No-one else is likely to tell you that you are allowed to! Don't just accept it. Challenge it.

- Remember De Bono's Six Hat Technique. Especially challenge the facts. Ask to see where it says, "NQTs always cover for absent staff before others" or "NQTs always take senior staff their lunch on a tray." (My experience as a new teacher in 1968; I hope that things have changed!)

- Consider Kobasa's three Cs of successful and content professionals (Kobasa, 1985, in Bloomfield, 1997). Are you paying enough attention to all of these areas?
  - **Commitment** to self, job and family. Note: not one or two but all three!
  - **Control** of your life. Not easy as a teacher in the new millennium!
  - **Challenged** not threatened by change. Depends how rapid!

Avoiding stress by deflecting it

"Some changes are so slow that you don't notice them. Some changes are so fast that they don't notice you."

I don't believe that humans were designed for the current pace of life and the current pace of change. In the wild, animals cope with stress by fight or flight or playing dead. None of these options looks particularly appealing to teachers, especially in the classroom! Some teachers have a tendency to create conflict, use verbal aggression, sarcasm and put-downs. These strategies may help them to cope with stress, but they increase the pupils' stress levels and are not conducive to learning. This means that teachers need to look for other ways of deflecting rather than repressing stress, both in and out of the classroom (See also Chapter 9):

- Say No. Be assertive. Use the 'broken record' technique of repeating your view clearly and politely.

- Work with your friends.

- Help and listen to others.

- Project a professional image right from the start.

- Be honest. Tell them how their behaviour really makes you feel.

- Be well prepared or over-prepared but prepared to be flexible or change. You will cope much better with transitions.

- Ask for help and advice. Then wait and listen to the answer or response.

- Try to be patient with yourself and others. We all make mistakes.

- Learn from your mistakes, then put them behind you and move on.

- Use significant events to help you to focus on what is important.

- Don't try to evaluate and reflect on everything. There's too much!

- Form a self-help NQT group which meets each week or month in a local hostelry. Form an NQT team to play mixed hockey, darts, pool, quiz, boules, or anything.

- Develop or extend your hobbies and interests. Involve yourself in learning and doing new things. (Mine are walking, pantomime, music, yoga, cooking and aromatherapy!)

- Enjoy the fellowship of others. This is not a luxury; it is an essential unless you are a hermit or dislike the company of others. Make time for this.

- Set aside time or find things to do that you find relaxing. As long as it makes a break, a space for you at home and work then that is fine. Mine include washing up and chatting to my eldest daughter. Yours could be walking or cycling to school and back home, walking the dog, playground duty, supervising the school chess team on away games, reading a book or magazine (hide it behind TES or an educational journal), weeding, playing a computer game or even ironing! These have all worked for me at various times. It's no good if you hate doing it. For me, this is swimming in chlorine filled swimming pools with grotty changing rooms!

- Volunteer for things you like doing and get rid of things you don't like doing (swap-shop timetabling).

- Work at your best time of day, in your best environment.

Using stress positively

A bit of stress, the adrenaline rush, is not always a bad thing. Performers get nervous. Challenge can be a great motivator. Anthony Robbins in *Unlimited Power* asks us "What would you do if you knew you could not fail?" So what is stopping you from making a start on that now, today?

Organising your classroom

The furniture

Essentially, you are making a fresh start in what was someone else's class. Don't be afraid to rearrange the classroom to how you want it. Experiment and get the children involved in planning the best use of the space you have. Get rid of redundant furniture but ask the headteacher and/or the caretaker's advice first. Simple things like tightening or replacing screws and bolts or replacing missing stoppers on chair legs can make a significant improvement to your environment. Badly fitting doors can usually easily be repaired; worn wooden surfaces can be sanded and re-varnished. Make the caretaker your friend. Over the years, caretakers have 're-cycled' all sorts of things in my direction. Go skip hunting in a posh area. Ask for more furniture if you really need it, but be wary of the room becoming overcrowded.

Aim for flexibility rather than rigidity. Balance open shelving with cupboards with doors. Get locks fitted if you feel it is necessary. When was your room last decorated? Get it put on someone's priority list. Talk to the teacher governor.

Are there any health and safety issues, such as splintered wood, broken edges or unsafe floors with missing or uneven tiles or flooring? You are responsible now for your area. Talk to the health and safety representative. In that role, I achieved more bricks and mortar improvements than years of asking politely ever brought me. Play the health and safety card, but don't overplay it. Remember that someone somewhere has to pay. Can you brighten up the space cheaply and safely? Can parents help? Talk to the PTA via the headteacher. Make the place look good, feel good and do you good; a safe and stimulating learning environment.

The resources

Have a clean out in the 'honeymoon period'. You may be able to get new resources whilst you are a new face. The honeymoon period is the time to ask politely for resources which you feel you need to do your job well. Make a list and prioritise it. Keep working at the list and updating it. After a few years, you will surprise yourself at how well you have done. If you don't ask, you won't get. Don't be put off by negativity; remember that drops of water can wear away stone.

Go to teachers who appear well resourced and ask their advice. What strategies did they use? Remember that OFSTED is charged with reporting on how well the school is delivering value for money. Put up an argument that the resources you need will be well used to improve children's learning, to ensure their progress and to improve the school's effectiveness. Say what criteria you will use to judge the effectiveness of the new resources you are asking for. Make major items part of the school's development plan.

Think out from scratch what might be best where. Think about how often they are used and by whom; paint brushes near the sink, powder paint away from it, everyday equipment and resources easily to hand but secure as you would like. Find out what your budget is and when your budget is due for review in the School Development Plan. See if you can find money for good quality boxes to store equipment and materials in, clearly labelled. Accessible equipment and resources will help your pupils to become independent learners.

Other adults in the classroom

You are the teacher now and must work with and often deploy other adults in the room. The management of other adults, classroom assistants, parent helpers, special needs teachers, NNEB students, students on teaching placements or work experience is a growing responsibility, especially for primary teachers. Ask them what they need to get started, keep going, and help the children to progress. Make time to talk to them, brief them about what you are trying to achieve, give and ask for feedback. What advice can they give you? What would they like to be able to do? Are there staff development opportunities that you could help them make use of? Ask on their behalf. Look out for suitable guidebooks such as the recent NNS *Numeracy Guide for Classroom Assistants*.

The pupils

The children and you need space, so make room for them. Children, like adults, are highly territorial, but they behave like any young primates or mammals in the wild. They need to become your 'gang', you need to be the 'pack leader'. Realise that you must address their primitive 'Reptilian' brain's needs before they will be ready to work (See Chapter 7). You and they also need to sort out the logistics for things like bags, wet coats, PE kit and lunch boxes. Many primary and secondary classrooms were not designed with these items in mind. If yours was, then you are lucky. Do not let wet coats or lunch boxes dominate your teaching time.

The classroom is a space which you and they must share. Try to encourage their ownership of the space, their suggestions for the problems and potential solutions. I have found that school as a workplace generates plenty of logistical problems which children can, do and will solve, given a chance. A well-written letter from a group of pupils about lunchbox storage or lack of lockers will get you further than storming into the staffroom and sounding off about it!

Chapter 4

MANAGING BEHAVIOUR

 You've got to accentuate the positive to eliminate the negative...

Chapter contents:

- **Strategies for managing behaviour in your new school**

- **Understanding your pupils' needs**

- **Developing your behaviour management strategies**

- **Behaviour and behaviourism: positive teaching**

- **Dealing with bullying**

Strategies for managing behaviour in your new school

You must have a set of strategies thought out before you start teaching. These strategies should be based on the school's behaviour policy, good classroom practice that you have observed, your own ideas and your own way of doing things.

Know your pupils

When discussing the class with the previous class teacher, make a note of particular children's needs, difficulties or problems. Be very careful about confidentiality. Get to know pupils as individuals. What interests and hobbies do the children have? Their skills, knowledge and interests may surprise you. Be positive and build relationships.

Know the routines

Find out about the school's routines for:

- arriving at school in the morning;
- going to and from assembly;
- going to the toilets;
- using the school grounds at breaks;
- going into class;
- moving around the school;
- wet break times;
- dinner times.

Which rewards and sanctions should you use?

Read the school's behaviour and anti-bullying policies. Make a list of the strategies used by the last class teacher or your induction tutor. Note what are the rewards for good work or good behaviour. What are appropriate sanctions for major and minor offences and in what order should they be used? What should you not use as a sanction? Add any things that you like to use or have seen elsewhere. Mark any strategies that you feel uncomfortable about using. Discuss these with a your induction tutor.

How should you use rewards and sanctions?

You should now have a set of strategies for reward and sanction. This should make you feel one step ahead. Try to praise five children for every child you tell off. Use constructive and appropriate sanctions. Try to be consistent, keep your promises and do what you say you will. Many teachers discuss and welcome the pupils' involvement in making the class rules. Make the agreed rules well known, repeat them, insist on them, and reinforce them. Display them in your classroom. Explain why they are necessary and important. Keep explaining; be persistent.

Do all you can to avoid:
- Humiliating   it breeds resentment;
- Shouting   it diminishes you;
- Over-reacting   the problem will grow;
- Sarcasm   it damages the child;
- Blanket punishment   the innocent will resent you;
- Public confrontation   it is better to diffuse the situation quietly.

Do all you can to:
- Use humour   it builds bridges;
- Keep calm   it releases tension;
- Listen   it earns respect;
- Respect pupils   it builds integrity;
- Expect good behaviour   it raises pupils' expectations;
- Praise good behaviour   it reinforces the positive.

Understanding your pupils' needs

In order to manage your pupils, it is important to understand their needs. What do your pupils need? Here is an overview of some theories of human need.

Kelmer-Pringle, 1974 – Basic Needs for Young Children
- **love and security;**
- **new experiences;**
- **praise and recognition;**
- **responsibility.**

Purkey, 1970 – Creating a Positive Self-image and Enhancing Self-esteem
- **challenge:** high expectations, relevant;
- **freedom:** to make decisions, from threat;
- **respect:** for self, for others;
- **warmth:** safe and supportive environment, commitment;
- **control:** clearly established routines, firm and consistent guidance;
- **success:** praise, support and encouragement rather than blame.

The dreadful converse; destroying belief in self and denigrating self-esteem:

- lack of challenge: boredom due to low expectations or irrelevant tasks;
- lack of freedom: indecision and helplessness due to an oppressive atmosphere;
- lack of respect: for self and others, producing a negative sub-culture;
- lack of warmth: unsafe, hostile and unsupportive environment;
- lack of control: due to inconsistent, unclear or absent routines and guidance;
- lack of success: insecurity due to blame.

Maslow, 1954 – Hierarchy of Human Needs

• **Intellectual:** self-actualisation, knowledge and understanding	**top**
• **Social:** love, belonging, acceptance by peers, self-esteem	**middle**
• **Primary Personal:** food, shelter, clothes/warmth, sleep, security	**base**

The learner's primary personal and social needs must be satisfied before intellectual needs can even begin to be met. I have adapted Maslow's list and turned the order round to deal with the most essential first. Before children can learn they must be:

- happy and healthy;
- warm and safe;
- belonging and contributing;
- respected and expected to learn.

Health and happiness

Children will not learn readily if they cannot hear or see properly or if they are suffering from coughs, colds or something more serious. Find out what you can about the children in your class. Observe them as they come into the class. Do they look healthy and happy? Their sadness might be temporary (a minor injury, an argument, a lost coat or broken toy) and require your sympathy and understanding. Or it might have serious and long-term implications (death of a relative, physical, mental or sexual abuse, bullying, or problems at home). Ask for help from your induction tutor, the headteacher or whoever is responsible for pastoral care.

Security and feeling safe

Is the classroom a pleasant place to be? Is there enough 'personal space' for all? My best primary classroom was warm, cosy, a bit old fashioned, and had lots of plants, gerbils, stick insects, plenty of books, games and interesting things to work with. We worked hard to keep everything labelled, tidy and cared for. We had clearly defined routines for every day of the week. As well as the school rules, we made up our own class rules, which we debated carefully so that everyone knew why we had decided to adopt them. Establish rules, boundaries and routines and explain why. Look and act as if you know what you are doing. Even in an emergency, children will trust and follow you if you appear calm and confident even if inside you are terrified. Always ask yourself 'Is this safe for children?'

Encourage team-building

We all belong to and aspire to belong to a number of different groups or teams. Make the children proud to be in your class and happy with the group they are in. Use different groupings for different activities. Don't be afraid to move the furniture for specific activities or rearrange the groupings to secure a better working atmosphere. Don't forget to praise the whole class or a particular group if they deserve it.

Building individual self-esteem

Many consider this the key factor for success. Praise individuals by name. Praise everyone in turn. Get to know what makes individuals tick if you can. Catch them being good. Encourage realistic competition with themselves. Promise them that they will improve if they work at it, follow your guidance and believe in themselves. Programmes such as Highscope (See the Bibliography) work hard to encourage self-discipline and self-esteem. Circle time or tutorial time can give everyone the chance to be heard, valued and shine.

Developing knowledge, understanding and the motivation to work

When the child's personal and social needs are satisfied, you will be able to teach them, and try to satisfy their intellectual needs, provided you can motivate them. Even better, can they motivate themselves or even perhaps motivate you?

Developing your behaviour management strategies

'I've come to the frightening conclusion that I am the decisive element in the classroom. It's my personal approach that creates the climate. It's my daily mood that makes the weather. As a teacher, I possess a tremendous power to make a child's life miserable or joyous. I can be a tool of torture or an instrument of inspiration. I can humiliate or humour, hurt or heal. In all situations, it is my response that decides whether a crisis will be escalated or de-escalated and a child humanised or dehumanised.'

Haim Ginott

What beginner teachers tend to do

Here are some observations about new teachers. Beginner teachers:
- were unclear about classroom rules, either their own or those of other teachers in the school;
- did not use terms such as 'right' and 'proper' when talking about rules;
- were unaware of the huge collective effort the staff had put into starting off the school year;
- made less use of eye contact and were very conscious of themselves being looked at;
- often neglected early infringements of class rules which then escalated into larger problems;
- concentrated on their preparation of lesson content rather than rules and relationships.

Consider your school situation and the class(es) you teach. Which of these are relevant to you?

What experienced teachers tend to do

More experienced teachers:
- were usually very clear about their classroom rules;
- did not hesitate to describe what they thought was 'right' and 'proper';
- were conscious of the massive effort needed to establish relationships with a new class;
- used their eyes a great deal to scan the class or look at individuals;
- were quick to deal publicly with any infraction of their rules;
- were more 'formal' than usual;
- were especially brisk and businesslike;
- established their presence in the corridor before the class even entered the room;
- introduced themselves formally, but, as if to temper the formality, gave incidental details of their personal background.

Do any of these reflect your classroom practice yet? Can you develop them over the induction year?

What the Elton Report believes is 'good practice'

'Some of the clearest messages are that teachers should:
- know their pupils as individuals, knowing their names, personalities, interests and friends;
- plan and organise both the classroom and lesson to keep pupils interested and minimise the opportunity for disruption. This requires attention to such detail as furniture layout, grouping of pupils, matching of work to ability, being enthusiastic;
- be flexible in order to take advantage of unexpected events (e.g. the appearance of the window cleaner or wasp mid-lesson);
- continually observe or 'scan' the behaviour of the class;
- be aware of and control their own (teacher's) behaviour, including stance and tone of voice;

- model the standards of courtesy they expect from pupils;
- emphasise the positive, including praise for good behaviour as well as for good work;
- make the rules for classroom behaviour clear to pupils from the first lesson and explain why they are necessary;
- make sparing and consistent use of reprimands. Be firm rather than aggressive, target the right pupil, criticise the behaviour not the person, be fair and consistent, avoid sarcasm and idle threats;
- make sparing and consistent use of punishments. Don't punish the whole group.'

Which do you need to develop over your induction year? Which are a priority for your class this term?

What do children want in a good teacher?

A good teacher should:
- keep order, and be firm without being severe, overwhelming or frightening;
- explain clearly, and help pupils to learn;
- be fair, do not pick on pupils, have favourites, or punish unjustly;
- be friendly and good-humoured, approachable and have a laugh;
- be interesting, provide a variety of stimulating work and use pupils' ideas.

Will your pupils recognise you as a good teacher?

Classroom atmosphere

What attitudes do you need to encourage a more positive self-image in children?
- Be calm, accepting and supportive, rather than threatening, grim and sarcastic.
- Show an interest in each child and value each one.
- Show confidence in the ability of a child to do the task set.
- Have clear values and a well-structured environment.
- Give a positive image of a child to their parent(s) or guardian.
- Be genuine rather than putting on a 'front'.
- Talk to the children about non-school matters. Be positive and realistic about yourself.
- Learn to recognise what to like, respect and accept about yourself.

Are your personality and attitudes in tune with creating and maintaining a classroom atmosphere which encourages a more positive self-image in children? Discuss these points with your induction tutor.

Using the five stage 'I' message

I have always found that giving learners a choice involves them more in their learning. An interesting trend can be found in the continuum from 'hoping' that they will do what you want, to 'forcing' them to do what you want, neither of which offer much choice, if any.

Hope ═══ Imply ═══ Suggest ═══ Ask ═══ Tell ═══ Demand/Threaten ═══ Force

Notice that the maximum choice rests in the centre when you suggest, ask or, even better, discuss which particular response might be appropriate for a particular task. Alistair Smith (1998) suggests that:

'A five stage 'I' message for dealing with problem behaviour starts with a positive recognition, then:

stage one:	describe the problematic behaviour, "When you…"
stage two:	describe the effects of the behaviour
stage three:	state how it makes you 'feel'
stage four:	describe the behaviour you want
stage five:	ask the person how they feel about your request

The person is not the problem. It is the behaviour which is the problem. The same person will behave differently in different contexts and may behave differently at different times with the same teacher. Remind them of this when you deal with the behaviour.'

Dealing with attention-seeking behaviour

You may find it useful to try to classify the types of attention-seeking behaviour in your classroom. We all use strategies to cope with life. As adults, we often use different strategies when we are with different people or in different situations; with our parents, our partners, friends, colleagues and with our children; at home, on holiday, in the pub, at a concert or a match, and at school.

A classification of attention seekers	Active	Passive
Constructive	Teacher's helper	Pleasantly helpless
Destructive	Class clown	Stubborn

Sometimes what we experience in the classroom does not respond well to giving attention. What are we to do and how can we tell? In an old study (Druikers, 1957; see also MacManus 1989), it is suggested that we try to diagnose what the pupil is after by considering our reaction and their reaction to this. I have found this simple technique very helpful, easy to learn and use and often effective.

How to diagnose and react to attention, power and revenge

A Observe your own feelings. You are probably reacting the way the pupil wants you to.

B Observe the pupil's reaction to your correction. Keep it to the minimum. Don't over-react.

C Take control. Reject your normal impulse and respond as suggested opposite.

	A Your feelings	B Pupil's response	C Your response
Attention	Irritation	Stops momentarily – – – – – – –	Give attention on your terms (the minimum). Use praise when appropriate.
Power	Challenged	Continues =============	Empower them. Give them responsibility, but on your terms. Keep them guessing.
Revenge	Outraged	Escalates >>>>>>>>>>>>>	Don't fight it. It probably belongs to another time, place and person. Go and ask for help.

Behaviour and behaviourism: positive teaching

'The ideal teacher tries to be optimistic, defends, understands, and allows for difficult pupils, avoids confrontation, respects pupils' dignity and engages them informally in a sympathetic and sharing climate.'

MacManus, 1989

Positive teaching

Merrett and Wheldall (1990) are concerned with positive teaching methods to manage pupils' social behaviour, in the belief that effective classroom behaviour management is a necessary condition for learning to take place. I certainly do not agree with all that they say, but I have found that behaviourist methods do work when trying to understand and deal with children's behaviour. This may well be because the Reptilian brain is the one we are trying to appeal to (survival, rote behaviours, defending your territory, showing off, attention-seeking, preening, group hierarchies and keeping your place in the pecking order). We cannot get on with the teaching without a working environment.

The five principles of positive teaching (Merrett and Wheldall, 1990)

Teaching is concerned with the observable. It is vital to observe children's behaviour carefully in order to analyse it and decide on what action if any, to take. This behaviour can be recorded using clear notes or a tally system.

Almost all classroom behaviour is learned. Unacceptable behaviour can be unlearned and appropriate behaviour can take its place.

Learning involves change in behaviour. Only when we observe changes in behaviour can we be sure that learning has taken place. Children are seen to complete their work on time and answer questions. This is a classic behaviourist objectives model. These changes can be recorded.

Behaviour changes as a result of its consequences. We all learn to repeat those behaviours that we find pleasurable or which result in reward of some kind. We avoid those behaviours that result in unpleasant experiences or punishment.

Behaviours are influenced by classroom contexts. The same class can behave differently with different teachers, or in different surroundings, in the same room with the same teacher but with different seating arrangements or different resources.

Merrett and Wheldall assume that teaching is about bringing about changes in behaviour in the classroom. This can be achieved by pupils' interactions with the teacher, each other and their environment. The events that both precede and follow the required behaviour are also of great importance. This is one reason why transitions are often problematic for new teachers.

Developing effective classroom strategies (Merrett and Wheldall, 1990)
Positive teaching is concerned with identifying and increasing appropriate behaviour. Good behaviour needs to be noticed and rewarded with a specific reinforcer. Reinforcers must be applied contingently; immediately, consistently and abundantly.

Contingently
The reinforcer must follow the particular behaviour every time but not at any other time. The reward is contingent on the specific behaviour of the pupil. It is not available otherwise, e.g. a merit for clearing up in time.

Immediately
The pupil should not have to wait for reward or praise. Both can and should be given immediately. For example, a class sticker for moving to or from the hall quietly; four stickers will result in a free choice activity for the whole class. Too often in education, the reward is either too far into the future to interest the pupil or else it is not relevant to them.

Consistently
Consistency is essential if the pupil is to be able to work out how the rule system works. Often, pupils are disruptive because they are not treated consistently either at home or at school. Children are right to demand a fair system; one which is reliable, predictable and sensible, and is practised by all of the teachers in the school.

Abundantly
Catch them being good; make sure that you reward the specific behaviour generously at first. Later, once the desired behaviour is occurring often enough, you will have to reduce the reward in frequency and immediacy until it is extinguished but the good behaviour is still in place. Then it is time to move on to a new target. This 'fading' must be not be started too soon or occur too quickly. Severe and speedy 'fading' might well feel like inconsistency.

Observe classroom behaviour carefully, examine the problem, define it clearly, state your aims and the means you intend to use to bring about the changes your require. Teachers must be able to justify their actions in terms of the long-term benefits for their pupils. A good place to start might be with the school's mission statement. Anything which negates that should be considered inappropriate. Anything which enhances it should be encouraged. Can you think of things that might annoy you but are not wrong? What constitutes inappropriate behaviour?

- Does it interfere with the child's own learning?
- Does it interfere with the learning of others?
- Does it prevent you or other adults from getting on with their job of explaining, instructing, modelling, demonstrating, organising, coaching and so on?

Focusing on appropriate classroom behaviour

Praise and reward should only follow appropriate work or behaviour. Whenever possible, we must try not to reinforce negative behaviours. Children who demand attention will get it in a negative way by being punished. Try to build a translator in your head, which converts negative statements into positive. For example, instead of "Stop picking your nose, Henry!", why not try "Henry, would you like to use a tissue?" Instead of "Stop making so much noise, Class 3!", try "Thank you, green group, for working quietly". We naturally find fault. Somehow we must turn it into praise. We need to 'catch them being good'. Hard as it may seem, it is often best to ignore trivial unwanted behaviour, but at the same time this only works if we reward good behaviour and get on with the lesson and keep the work interesting. Catching them being good demands skilled observation of even the slightest improvement.

Find out what pupils' are interested in. What do they consider a reward? Give them attention, but when you want to and on your terms not theirs. What needs doing in the class? Might they be able to help you? Punish by removing privileges. It must be something they actually value. Try to avoid public confrontation. Talk to the pupil quietly at the end of the lesson when the rest of the class has gone out but keep the door open.

Circle time or tutorial time can be used to explain or develop rules for positive behaviour. If the pupils develop these themselves then they are much more likely to understand them and stick to them. Pupils must be aware of what the rules are, why they are there, and what happens if they are not followed. Then they choose to obey or disobey them in full knowledge of the consequences, which should be applied fairly. Children have a right to expect a fair system.

Work on saving time and giving it back to the class, for example timing how long it takes to get ready for PE for example. Do you like PE? Would you like to spend more time doing it? It is easy if we spend less time getting ready. Record, graph or plot the times each week and see how they improve. Try to maintain them at a good level. The same applies to clearing up at the end of a lesson. Would you like a longer break? Then get ready sooner. I argued with my class one year that if we saved five minutes each lesson we could earn ourselves three whole days in the summer term. We used it to clear a local stream of rubbish with help from the local council who provided rubber gloves, bags and a skip. We surveyed the river and spent three memorable days in the sun. The time was well earned and well used.

Try to provide challenging and interesting tasks in an environment that is non-threatening and in which the pupils believe that they can succeed. Being afraid and knowing that they will fail or be ridiculed is not a recipe for learning. Be welcoming. Greet each person in turn as they enter the classroom. Try to say something positive if you can, welcome them by name. I use this to notice if pupils are in a good mood, feeling unwell or looking tired.

Enhancing praise and reprimands

Find out what rewards are likely to work by observing pupils when they have freedom of choice and by asking them what they like best. Free choice of activity, extra break time, longer games sessions, public praise and a positive letter home are some rewards that have found favour in the past. Interestingly, pupils surveyed did not consider being told off and being sent out to be effective sanctions. They valued free time and a positive letter home. So their teachers' normal sanctions and rewards did not match theirs. If you are considering devising your own set of rewards and sanctions, ensure that they fit in with the school's behaviour policy. Discuss them with your induction tutor.

Setting appropriate and effective classroom rules

Praise and rewards should be contingent on appropriate work and behaviour. They need to be attainable and in a reasonable time. The best rules are those that pupils have developed and discussed with their teacher. They should fit into the school's framework. The simplest I've come across is from a primary school in St Helier. 'We care. We share'. Make only a few rules, perhaps three or four, which are phrased positively rather than a page full of 'Thou shalt nots'. Make the rules specific so that everyone knows if they are being kept or broken. It is better to include the word 'try' in your classroom rules. Everyone can at least try. You can aim for things to keep getting better by moving the goal posts, albeit slowly and only when the required behaviour or work patterns are established. Get rid of a rule and add a new one. This provides a good opportunity for praise, reward and discussion. This is like Total Quality Management in the classroom. Keep striving for perfection.

Dealing with bullying

All school staff have a responsibility to be alert to the problem of bullying. Make sure that you have read the school's anti-bullying policy. Report all incidents of bullying. Talk to your induction tutor if you feel you need advice.

Why bother about bullying?

- Bullying makes children unhappy.
- Children who are being bullied are unlikely to concentrate fully on their schoolwork.
- Some children avoid being bullied by not going to school.
- Children who observe unchallenged bullying behaviour may copy this anti-social behaviour.
- Schools which do take action against bullying build a reputation as effective caring schools.
- Little bullies grow into big bullies.

Some questions worth discussing

- What is bullying? What causes people to bully one another?
- How does it feel to be bullied or to bully?
- What are the effects of bullying behaviour on the bullied? On the bully and the bystanders?
- What would our school be like if bullying behaviour was acceptable?
- Why should we try not to bully one another? What can we do to stop bullying?
- What moral dilemmas do we face when we are confronted by bullying behaviour?

How can bullying be tackled?

- By the whole school, teaching and non-teaching staff as well as the children themselves, parents and governors developing a whole-school policy which they have contributed to and own.

Schools which successfully counter bullying have a whole-school policy which aims to:
- develop staff awareness;
- involve parents and the community;
- promote creative and enjoyable playground activities;
- work with both the bullied and the bully;
- encourage children to support each other;
- deal with bullying as part of the school curriculum.

What can I do?

- Become more aware of bullying, the bully and the bullied. Observe children at play. What constitutes bullying?
- Find out about the school's policy for behaviour and bullying. Talk to staff, children and parents.
- Learn and teach games which children can play.
- Use Circle Time and discussion of incidents as they arise to help children become more aware of their actions and how they can help themselves and one another.

Based on Bullying: Don't Suffer in Silence, *DFE, 1994*

Chapter 5

ASSESSING AND EVALUATING TEACHING AND LEARNING

I aim to help the NQT to become a reflective practitioner, not to depend on me. We talk about what has gone right so that they can build on the successes and the positives, then we can unpick what didn't go quite so well.

Induction tutor

Chapter contents:

- **What did they learn today?**

- **Keeping and using an assessment file**

- **Making assessments**

- **Different forms of record-keeping**

- **The cycle of planning, teaching and evaluating**

- **The quality and effectiveness of your own teaching**

What did they learn today?

You will find yourself asking yourself such questions as:

- Did my presence in the classroom today make a significant difference in what the pupils learnt?

- How do I know? How do they know?

- How can I assess my pupils' achievement, progress and potential?

- How can I assess my own progress?

The following sections should help you to answer these difficult questions.

Pupils' attainment

The word attainment can refer to:

- the capability of the pupil in relation to national expectations;

- the capability of the pupil in relation to their peers in their class or age group;

- how a pupil achieves in relation to their individual targets, including those specified by an individual education plan (IEP);

- what a pupil knows, understands and can do.

Only the pupil's teacher has sufficient knowledge and professional skill to determine:

- whether a pupil is generally able to perform in relation to the level descriptions contained in the Attainments Targets;

- whether this level of performance could be said to be appropriate and within expectations (or outstanding for a pupil of low ability, or inadequate for a pupil of high ability).

Pupils' progress: "Could do better"

Attainment does not necessarily signify progress. Pupils might be doing work that is far too easy for them, with little or no challenge. Pupils are expected to make progress when they attend school. It could be that they will make progress irrespective of what the teacher does. That isn't acceptable. All of us who choose to teach and who are paid to teach should make a difference. It's in the area of your making a difference that the issue of progress arises.

The extent to which a pupil can be said to be making progress is evident when they:

- display a new insight;

- offer new ways of thinking;

- display new knowledge;

- demonstrate new skills;

- display changing attitudes;

- demonstrate and articulate new strategies;

- question existing knowledge, extending their horizons;

- can do or say something that they could not do or say before.

You may also detect changes of attitude to self, to others and to work, especially when there is a deep personal involvement and engagement with a task; a 'feeling' for the subject. You should therefore try to notice and make use of pupils' developing knowledge, skills and attitudes. Pupils can also record some of their developments in the artefacts they make, performances they give, and in spoken and in written presentations.

Keeping and using an assessment file

Ask about the school's procedures for gathering assessment evidence and follow the school's policy for assessment, recording and reporting. Your file could take various forms (see the later section on record-keeping):

- a book with a double page for each pupil, which helps to keep the pupil as the focus, and where any relevant observations can be jotted;

- a file with sections for core subjects including ICT, foundation subjects and RE;

- a file or folder with a section for each pupil with relevant sub-headings;

- a mark book divided into sections for different classes or units of your subject(s).

Quality is preferable to quantity. Observe and collect brief but pertinent data. The purpose of keeping a file is to bring together evidence from a range of sources that inform you about the pupil. Sources can include:

- observations in different contexts so you are informed about the pupil's knowledge, skills and attitudes in a variety of situations and groupings;

- notes from discussions with pupils;

- making accurate professional judgements derived from assessing pupils' practical work and recorded written responses in books and on worksheets.

Individual and group observations of pupils can focus on what pupils are actually capable of doing and saying.

Recording the date that the assessment was carried out allows you to review accumulated data so that you can compare dates and the pupil's achievement or attainment. By having evidence that a pupil could not do something easily in January, but can do it with ease in March, you have evidence of progress that you can report to the pupil and their parents/carers.

An assessment file can be used in different ways:

- It helps you plan future lessons so that you can provide what pupils need.

- Notes made as a result of observations should provide you with valuable information when talking informally and formally with parents, other relevant adults and the pupil.

- You will be better informed to assess the pupils in terms of NC level descriptors, the core skills and literacy and numeracy objectives.

- You will be able to use your notes when it comes to writing reports.

Making assessments

When you collect books in for marking, use the school's marking policy. When you mark the books of a target group that you have closely observed you can write detailed comments about:

- what they got right;

- how/why they did well;

- mistakes they made, described in words;

- why their work is wrong, clearly explained;

- how they could improve.

Don't forget that parents will see your comments. They will be in a better position to help their child if they've got your explanations and suggestions for improvements to read when the book goes home or when they come into school.

Using tests

You can devote short periods to a test that covers a part of the work that you've taught.

The test could be entirely informal and oral. Sit for 10 minutes with the pupils together in a group in exactly the same way that you would for starting any other lesson. Ask them to tell you anything they can remember about the topic. Don't get annoyed when they don't all remember. Don't turn it into a teaching lesson where you start explaining the 'real answer' to your original question; just genuinely enquire. When you get an incorrect answer, try asking generally to the class "Is that right? Is that what everybody thinks?" Gather the range of answers and write them all on a flipchart as the pupils give them to you. Don't give away your thoughts. Ask for explanations of each answer. Look out for confusion and misunderstood ideas. Note them down and move on to other questions. Later on, away from the pupils, review their responses and make an assessment on the depth and range of understanding demonstrated by the test. You can also evaluate the effectiveness of your questioning and your ability to probe their understanding.

A more formal test could be some typical questions that you expect pupils to answer successfully. It is better to give three short tests to different groups with the work matched closely to their ability than one test for everyone. If you can, mark the work with the pupils. Ask individual pupils how they tackled the problem. It is better to give five problems than 20 because this gives you more time to spend afterwards looking at pupils' mistakes and going over misconceptions with the class or with groups. There is helpful information on pupils' errors and misconceptions in English, maths and science on the CD-ROM *Assessing your Needs* (TTA, 1998).

A basic aim of education should be to demonstrate and promote success, so never give a test that you know a pupil is going to fail. Use the results of a test to help pupils improve.

A useful test is one that:

- gives you a better picture of what pupils actually know and can do;

- gives pupils feedback about whether they have worked correctly or not;

- shows pupils exactly what was wrong (e.g. lack of knowledge, misapplied method, incorrect strategy);

- leaves pupils knowing exactly how to do better in future, without feeling humiliated or embarrassed.

Other assessments

These can include a game or a quiz where you keep track of who has improved their factual knowledge and who needs further help and work. You can also use a pupil tracking-sheet during the lesson. Identify up to four pupils whose performance you can easily monitor during the lesson. Have a sheet for each pupil with a space at the top for name, date of birth, class and year group. Put a column for the date and a space in which to observe exactly what they can do. Include a final column for targets for development, in which to jot down what the next step will be for this pupil. It may be they need more practice to consolidate some shaky incomplete knowledge. It may be they need to move on to something more challenging. Observe the four pupils for a week. Next week identify four others. If four is too many make it two pupils at a time. Find what constitutes the briefest comment that still makes sense to you a month later and which their next teacher will be able to read and understand.

Different forms of record-keeping

Record-keeping is the formal collection and organisation of the information derived from assessment. See the table of different forms on pages 64 and 65.

Recording

Recording can take the form of informal notes on your observations or discussions. These can include the assessment of finished or unfinished artefacts and performances, designs, constructions, musical performances and physical performance, such as in dance, drama and PE. In each case, think about why you want to keep a record. What will you do with this record? What use will it be to the pupil's progress? Record-keeping can specifically relate the pupil's activity to attainment criteria. For example, achievement in swimming can be compared to the end-of-key-stage statements for PE.

Try using different coloured pens. Mark in a different colour each week. It is easy to see how much has been covered each week in your records and in pupils' books. Try colour coding the groups and using the codes in your plans and records. This works well when you have lots of different groups to organise. Try opening up the process so that the children record what they have done and how they feel about it. They could also record progress, what they thought went well and how they think they could improve. Targets can then be negotiated, made public and celebrated when they are achieved. This open record could be for the whole class on a pin board or stuck into individual books or a pupil's personal record book or file. Use 'pupil speak' or illustrated versions of targets for pupils to assess and record their own progress so that pupils with special needs are not excluded from taking part.

Concept maps

Concept maps can be used to:

- plan your teaching, provide a route through material and keep track of what has been done;

- show the structure of a topic, and the hierarchy, from the general to the specific;

- test and provide a record and evidence of what pupils know at the start of a topic;

- help them to negotiate meaning and add the concepts that they learn about during a topic;

- revise and re-test at the end of a topic to see how much they know, and where the gaps are.

A concept map consists of two types of things:

- Concepts, usually in boxes or drawn enclosed, form concept labels which can be words or symbols. These concepts can be ideas, events, nouns, perceived regularities or relationships.

- Links, usually drawn as lines, are made between the concepts, showing direction. These normally have linking words, such as verbs, written along them to make a statement. When you read the concepts and the words on the links in the direction of the arrow, a proposition is made. Does it make sense? Is it true?

You might find other kinds of mappings useful, such as spider charts and mind maps.

The cycle of planning, teaching and evaluating

Assessment and record-keeping play a role in the cycle of planning and preparation, implementation and evaluation. There are three broad stages:

1. Before teaching – planning and preparation

Review your previous lessons and other sources of assessment and ask yourself 'Based on what I know they can already do, what do these pupils need to do next? What do they now need from me?' Assessment is professional judgement or opinion based on evidence from a range of sources, including observations made during lessons and from written notes, comments written by you in pupils' books, tick sheets, notes to yourself and the results of tests that you've given them.

Plan for assessment opportunities. When you prepare each teaching plan, you need to identify an assessment you are going to make during the unit of work. Often, these assessments will be informal and targeted on a single small group. Usually, they will involve simple assessment activities, like a discussion with you, a game, or a worksheet that checks whether certain knowledge or skills have been acquired. For older pupils, they may involve more formal tests or sample exam papers.

2. During teaching – implementation

Teachers make informal assessments all the time. Listening to responses, deciding how to explain something and inviting a particular pupil to give an answer all involve you in making judgements about pupils' levels of understanding.

Some assessments are important enough to be recorded as a measure of attainment. When an individual pupil demonstrates a particular skill, or a group show they can apply some knowledge, it may be worth keeping a note. This is not the same as keeping a record of the completion of work. Both are important records to keep, but they are different forms of information. If the lesson goes well, a single assessment for the majority of pupils will be sufficient. However, a small number of pupils may not behave as you anticipated. In this case, individual assessments should be made of those pupils whose achievement is strikingly different from what you expected and the SENCO will be able to offer you advice.

At the start of your lesson, take some time to tell the pupils what constitutes good work and what exactly you will be looking for during the lesson. So that they know what good work is going to feel and look like, show them examples if you can.

During the last part of the lesson, ask pupils to describe something that they've learned. Remind them of the lesson objective and ask them about the strategies they've been practising. Accept that for some pupils, the most important thing might be that they've worked really well with a friend, or learned to share equipment without squabbling. Conclude by asking for suggestions about simple things that they could do in order to help themselves improve before the next lesson. If your informal assessments are in line with your expectations for the lesson, then record this as your assessment. Try to identify pupils who have significantly under-achieved as well as those who have amazed you, recording these individually.

Five different forms of record-keeping

	Advantages	Disadvantages	Reporting
Journal or book	All lessons appear in the sequence taught. Chronology is emphasised. Each lesson can be planned, and groups of pupils identified by writing their names together in clusters on the page for each lesson. Individual pupils' names can be highlighted afterwards, signalling who performed outside the general expectations you had for the group they were placed in.	Difficult to pick out individuals at a glance. Pupils can get lost if they don't stand out. You need to decide at the outset if it will be made public, if it is to be passed on to another teacher or written just for you. Who will need to see it? Headteachers often do.	Was commonly used to record project work. Provides a narrative. Action plans can be evident and easily reviewed and tracked. A good working record which others can see. Can be passed on and made available. Some schools display them openly and with pride.
Class list	Focuses on pupils through a (vertical) list of their names. Forces brief comments, codes or marks to be placed against each name. By drawing columns, chronology can be emphasised by dating a column. They don't have to be combined in a book but can be printed off a database as and when required. Can be used directly by pupils. Useful for indicating completion of a task, e.g. when a pupil ticks that they have used the computer this week. Useful for ensuring coverage of comments across the whole list (visually obvious when a name has nothing against it).	Not much space to put more than a mark, letter, symbol or sign. Personal, idiosyncratic and can be usefully coded like doctor's notes. Hard to pass on to another teacher. You need to develop your own codes, using ticks, crosses, o, !, ? and *, which mean something to you. Try A–E for achievement and 1–5 for effort.	You can read your codes, and notice trends over time. Whole schemes or programmes of study can be covered in a few pages. You can record aspects such as ICT, composition, handwriting or test results for one term on one sheet. You can read back your code. Try a class list in age order. Some use alphabetical order or the class listed in groups.
Individual cards	Compact and practical. Can be kept in box on or near teacher's desk/work area and filled in during some lessons or during non-teaching time. Helps develop memory and forces retention of information and selectivity. Requires brief, coded information. Encourages you to write only what you will want to know at a later time. Good for times when you have chosen a pupil to focus on. If you keep the card for the pupil you are interested in on the top of the bundle, you always know who to make notes on next. When complete, move the pupil's card to bottom of pile.	Problems when cards fill up. What to do when some pupils' cards are full and others not? Not always clear where to go to retrieve information. Superfluous information gets in the way and is an indicator of previously wasted time. Doesn't allow easy access to a specific pupil at any one time, so isn't easy to use if something memorable happens to three different pupils each lesson. Personal, idiosyncratic and cannot easily be passed on.	At a later date, can you read your remark/comment and recall clearly your reasons for writing it? A good comment brings the moment flooding back: it triggers the memories of the situation. Could your comments be used to: ● give clear feedback to the pupil? ● communicate precisely to another teacher? ● give a simple oral report to a parent?

	Advantages	Disadvantages	Reporting
Individual page per pupil	A single sheet for each pupil with name and group. Could be on coloured paper to show which group pupil is in. A column to show date when each comment was made. Two other columns for the actual observation and a second one for a specified target. Advantage is that when pupil meets the target some time later, it can be dated and ticked. Possible to track 3 or 4 pupils during a week. Sheets don't have to be confined to one subject so can contain comments (including behaviour) for the pupil for the week. Only have to make note of significant events, not trivia. At start of week, 3 or 4 pupils' sheets are brought to the front of the file with a card separating them from the rest of the class. At end of week, the sheets are put to the back of the file and the new ones revealed for the next week.	Temptation and external pressure to write everything about everybody. This is impossible and unhelpful. Some experienced teachers report being able to manage making notes of up to four target pupils during lesson time. Others report not being able to use this method at all. Therefore, it isn't a function of ability or skill but rather it's about where a teacher chooses and is able to put their energy during the lesson.	Very useful for tracking significant achievement. Pupils' progress can be reviewed and reported on formally and informally to other teachers, pupils and parents.

If the layout of the page matches the school report form, then writing reports is a relatively simple matter of transcription. |
| File with group lists | FA single sheet for each group with date that this particular grouping began and a list of names of those in the group at top of a single page. New pages are easy to add. If you keep your groupings fairly constant, then one sheet per group. Sheet for target group is brought to the front of the file, kept open on table, ready for notes to be made during the lesson or immediately afterwards. Note the general group response and any significant deviations up or down. A good system for mixed aged classes. | Tempting to write something about every pupil in group, but end up writing trivia because there's nothing necessary to write. If keeping records in this way is disruptive to your thinking during your lesson, then it's not the method for you. Other teaching skills must take priority. If you change your groups very frequently, this is not easy to maintain. | Group lists encourage focusing on a single group and are very useful if your teaching includes direct teaching to that group. If your schedule means you work with every group sometime during the week, then this means you can comment on a selection of pupils across all groups during a week. |

3.   After teaching – reviewing and evaluating

Use your assessments to help you to plan what to do next with these pupils. You might well have to record your assessment as part of a regular formal process that the school has adopted. Schools have to report pupils' attainment to parents at least once each year at a parents' meeting. Schools also have to make end-of-key-stage assessments and submit the results of these for publication. It is important that teacher assessments are of the highest quality and that they can be seen as being professionally sound, especially to those outside the profession. Using this cycle will ensure that they are.

The quality and effectiveness of your own teaching

During your induction year, you will be re-appraised against the original standards for QTS and assessed against a specific new set of induction standards. I believe that the standards should be used carefully to make a positive statement about what you are able to do. No teacher works at 100% effectiveness all the time so if you can do something then include it as one of the things you are competent to do. Not being able to do it all the time just means you're human like the rest of us. Why you don't display a professional competence more frequently is a matter for professional consideration.

Your induction tutor can help you to chart your professional development against the specific induction standards by using the 'traffic light system' (See Appendix A). This has been developed specifically so that consideration of teaching performance is a positive activity where potential for growth is identified, and blocks to your professional development can be shown in order to encourage reflective practice, help you to identify and plan for specific needs and complete your induction year successfully.

Part 2: Developing your teaching

Chapter 6

MODELS OF TEACHING

Listen to your induction tutor's advice, but use their ideas in your own way. Make your sessions together a two-way process. Learn from each other.   NQT

Chapter contents:

- ■ **Recognising your own dominant teaching and learning styles**

- ■ **Looking for good models of teaching**

- ■ **The importance of strategies in teaching and learning**

- ■ **Making links using bridging**

- ■ **Strategies for differentiation**

Recognising your own dominant learning and teaching styles

Do teachers teach the way they were taught rather than the way that they were taught to teach? Do we tend to regress to the teaching styles that we experienced as pupils? Are you aware that you tend to favour certain teaching styles whilst avoiding others? Does this depend on our own preferences for learning? How is this influenced by your dominant cognitive style? (See Chapter 8.)

Adult learning styles

Honey and Mumford (1992) describe four different modes for adult learners, based on the work of Kolb. Which of these learning styles matches yours?

- **Activists:** Those who enjoy the here and now, are dominated by immediate experiences and thrive on challenge but get bored with implementation and long-term consolidation.

- **Reflectors:** Those who stand back and ponder, collect data and analyse it, consider all possible angles and are cautious.

- **Theorists:** Those who are keen on basic assumptions, theories, principles and models; are rational and logical, detached and analytical; are able to assemble disparate facts into coherent theories. They like to make things tidy and fit.

- **Pragmatists:** Those who search out new ideas, experiment, brim with lateral thinking and see problems as new opportunities and challenges.

I have long held the view that many teachers are dominant left brain thinkers, whilst their pupils might prefer any one of a variety of cognitive styles (see Chapter 8). McCarthy (1987) reports that around 25% of the adult population are left dominant, 25% right dominant and 50% balanced left and right. If this can be extrapolated to the classroom, then a teacher using a dominant left brain style would perhaps satisfy 25% of the class all of the time, another 50% of the class 50% of the time and the remainder hardly ever. I remember some language teachers who could not imagine that learning could be composed of anything but reading, writing and talking, all of which are linear, usually logical and symbolic. Compare this to drawing, designing and making. Now ask yourself if art and design teachers are easy to identify in the staffroom? Why is this so? I particularly remember two art teachers with whom I have worked. They enthused pupils to produce superb work. Both teachers were colourful personalities outside and in.

If we can become aware of our own preferences, yet realise that the way we prefer to learn and perhaps teach might not be best suited to all the children in the class, then most of us are prepared to expand our repertoire for the sake of our pupils. If you are one of the lucky balanced ones, then you will know this already. What we want to achieve is balanced pupils who are capable of using both sides of their brain to advantage and also appreciate the way others think and act (De Bono, 1994).

Looking for good models of teaching

Find good models of teaching to base your practice on; try to understand them and make them your own. The induction programme requires you to develop a variety of teaching methods. You are expected to expand and create new learning opportunities with them. Look for new models of teaching to begin the cycle again. Do not be surprised or dismayed if it takes you a while to develop a new model of teaching. Keep watching, keep trying and keep reflecting.

Joyce *et al* (1997) suggest reading and talking about a 'new' model, watching and analysing demonstrations of it 20 times and then practising it in the classroom for about 50 hours. I would argue that if you see a new model twice, you should be able to notice some aspects that appeal and make sense to you. If you try them out four or five times, you will get a feel for some of the benefits. This should spur you on to take the model more seriously and find out more. The problem with this quicker approach is that, whilst it is more realistic, it is also more prone to the chance that you might dismiss a model without really understanding it. The most important thing to do is to talk to other teachers, particularly your induction tutor, about your teaching. If you can find a critical friend amongst the staff, then together you can develop your models of teaching.

Three approaches to developing your models of teaching

Finding new models

The very best place to find good models of teaching is in a classroom near you. If you can observe and discuss what you have seen with the person doing the teaching and the pupils doing the learning, then you have a great opportunity to make sense of what you see. You should be able to arrange to observe other teachers in other classes and perhaps other schools. The Numeracy Strategy specifies that teachers should give demonstration lessons which can be observed by groups of teachers from other schools as well as their own. Let us hope that this new initiative spreads and enthuses lots of teachers.

For some, videos provide an excellent source of teaching models. It is possible to watch them more than once, in your own time, to discuss what you see with others and try out the ideas before watching the video again. For example, the current videos relating to primary numeracy work provide short enough episodes, of about 10 minutes, to get a good idea of the different models and the way a numeracy session might look in a relatively short time. The ages of the children vary across KS1 and KS2 and the teachers range in age and experience. It is worth asking around for good examples of video material. Often, there is excellent material that can be recorded from *The Learning Zone* on BBC2 after midnight.

Using existing models

Use an existing model with which you feel comfortable in one particular subject. Then try it in a different subject, setting or context. For example, you could try role-play in:

- science, when pretending to be molecules, or for classification based on observation of characteristics;

- maths, with work on shape;

- English, with characters in a novel;

- design and technology, to help to define a problem to be solved;

- geography, for cause and effect in physical systems or as part of an environmental study;

- history, considering cause and effect;

- PE, to explain the rules of a game or define a sequence of movements;

- RE, to get more than one viewpoint or the pros and cons of a situation;

- music, to critically analyse a composition;

- PSHE or careers, to explore a given situation, empathise with people from a different place or culture or undertake mock interviews.

Combining models

Use two or more models with which you are familiar and comfortable in series or together. Sometimes new teachers dwell too long on models of teaching which they like. Their pupils become bored by just one approach and, while it may suit their teaching, it will not necessarily match the dominant learning style of all the pupils. One easy way out of this is to vary the models within one session. The different phases of a lesson; beginning; middle and end, might benefit from a variety of models. Often, a model that works at the start might work at the end as well. Try it. Use two different models one after the other. You might improve your classroom organisation by running two models at the same time. Look for models that don't necessarily require your attention or could be used by another adult in the room. Meanwhile, you can work with one or two groups using a teacher-intensive model. You probably do this already but might not have thought about it in this way. Keep looking, thinking and talking about models of teaching to anyone who will discuss them with you. Use the noting of significant events to help you to keep track of, focus and help you reflect on your models of teaching (see Chapter 3).

The importance of strategies in teaching and learning

Strategies can be general, such as planning or looking for patterns, or specific to a particular subject, for example in mathematics, doubling or using your knowledge of odds and evens to see if an answer is sensible.

General learning strategies might include:

- checking the facts and questioning the rules before you start;

- planning to complete the task in time, being systematic, using trial and error;

- sharing the workload amongst the group, taking on different roles to solve a problem;

- looking for your own repetitions, omissions or mistakes;

- sharing strategies and misconceptions with others;

- looking for patterns, making rules;

- checking that answers are sensible, comparing a range of responses;

- setting your own targets.

Specific mathematical learning strategies might include:

- knowing odds, evens, count on, count back, using number bonds to ten;

- starting with the largest number, knowing how to double, halve, near double, being able to use approximate, round up, round down, and estimate;

- finding the nearest ten or hundred, using divisibility rules;

- knowing that the order of operations matters for subtraction and division;
- knowing that when more than one operation is used there is a priority of the operations.

General teaching strategies might include:

- a meta-level strategy such as Plan, Do, Review;
- planning your teaching carefully;
- making your teaching and learning intentions clear at the start of the lesson;
- asking questions, open and closed, of the whole class and of individuals;
- involving all pupils by being interactive and well paced;
- giving instant feedback from whole-class interactive teaching;
- reviewing learning intentions at the end;
- making time to watch and listen to pupils;
- letting them take centre stage; it will give you a chance to catch your breath.

Specific teaching strategies in maths might include:

- making links between experience, language, pictorial representation and symbolic representation, e.g. practically partitioning 10 children into two groups;
- discussing what has happened, predicting the number in each group, then counting them to make sure;
- drawing or representing the different sets of complementary numbers with counters and recording the objects;
- writing mathematical statements, such as $7 + 3 = 10$;
- aiming to give children the fluency and confidence to use mental methods as a first and reliable resort.

An analogy for these strategies might be with tools for cooking, gardening or working on plumbing, wiring or car engines. Gardening and DIY programmes, watching the experts at work, seem very popular at present. The tools an artist uses such as pencils of different hardness and colour, brushes of different thickness and texture, paints of different colours and type such as water colour, oils or acrylic, different paper and other materials to work on and with might be better than we have at home. We need to learn to experiment with each one in turn, starting with something simple such as finger painting or drawing with a big wax crayon. Learning to use the tool is a skill. Deciding which tool to use, and where and when to use it is the strategy. Strategies can be exemplified with different resources. With experience, we learn to make different marks and develop our skill at using each one. In the same way, we can learn a range of strategies in any context, including mathematics or reading.

The importance of practice, 'simmering' (consolidating) and then extending

First of all, we must believe that we need to and should learn a new strategy. Next, we must practise it in some meaningful way. Then, we have to keep using it and applying it or else we will lose it. It doesn't really become a fully-fledged strategy at our disposal until we feel safe using it, know when and how to use it and feel some fluency and confidence. We also need to remember that it is available or else it will just sit there unused. Do you apply this strategy in your teaching?

The importance of having a range of strategies at our disposal

No matter what the endeavour or your age, if you have no strategies at all, then success could be a random event, and hard to learn from. We might, if we are very confident, just try anything and see what happens. This 'playfulness' remains important throughout our lives. It is sad to see how many of us reject it during childhood. We can learn from trial and error (trial and improvement), but I suspect that we already know something about the setting or something like it. Very young babies use grasping an object and putting it into their mouths as a strategy to find out if the object is edible and sense what it is like. A toddler confronted by a new garment will try to put it on. A stranger in a foreign country unable to speak the language will try signs, sounds, gestures or pointing to get what they want. A beginner teacher will sometimes try a carefully planned session based on how they were taught. If we have no strategies at all, we are somewhat at a loss to start. We can of course avoid learning new strategies altogether by using the single strategy of getting someone else to do it for us; 'learned helplessness'.

With one strategy we may succeed, but should the strategy fail we are at a loss again. Over reliance on one strategy leaves us powerless, without a choice when we most need to be empowered. Knowing how to say one word or play one note results in limited communication and expression. You can get started and with a few more words or notes you can actually choose how to express yourself. Not being able to express yourself or make yourself understood can cause intense frustration which can lead to anger and violence, as anyone who has witnessed the 'terrible twos' will agree, although not getting your own way plays a part in your development too.

The whole point of developing a range of strategies is that we can choose the most appropriate one to the circumstances. If the problem looks hard, then try a well-known and safe strategy. If we recognise the problem then we know what to do, and it is not then a problem unless we hit a snag. The most interesting problems require a range of different strategies in a particular order. This is true of making a cup of tea, rewiring a plug, getting dressed or undressed, assembling flat-packed kitchen units, servicing a car, delivering a baby or painting a watercolour landscape picture. A series of techniques is required, usually in a specific order. Often, there is that special trick or knack, such as wetting the paper, warming the pot, or adding a drop at a time.

With activities such as reading, numeracy and teaching, having a range of strategies which you prefer to use, and selecting those you find most appropriate, actually gives you more freedom, not less, and improves your efficiency. The fact that you neither know nor use all the possible strategies that have ever been used is not important. What is important is that you have enough different ones to allow you to use one if another fails and to give you that choice.

Making links using bridging

As an NQT or anyone starting anything for the first time, not having many or even any strategies really can cause a problem. Fortunately, general strategies can be applied to many human activities and are more or less transferable. There is debate about the extent to which a strategy can be transferred and certainly the situation or context in which the original strategy was learned is of importance. If the new situation is similar, then transfer is more likely.

Reuven Feuerstein (1983) calls the transfer of a strategy, such as planning, being systematic, checking the facts or looking at the pros and cons of a situation, bridging. For example, at the end of a session, in the plenary, links could be made to real life or cross-curricular issues. If you have been encouraging the learners to consider some skill such as looking for patterns, being systematic or setting their own targets, these skills could be bridged to other applications in other curriculum areas or in real life. How might planning, being systematic or setting your own targets be useful to you outside school?

Examples of bridging different boundaries

Specific strategies learned in one subject or situation can be bridged:

- across that subject, for example from arithmetic to algebra to geometry;
- across the curriculum, from one subject or discipline to another, such as from geography to mathematics or from music to dance.

General strategies learned in one subject or situation can be bridged:

- to life with your colleagues or peers at school, in the organisation or workplace;
- to life with your friends and family at home or in the wider world.

In each case, the fundamental questions to ask at the end of the learning experience are "What have I learned today and how can I use that elsewhere in the subject? In other subjects? In this organisation? In the rest of my life? At home and play outside work?" Another important consequence of this approach is to admit the value of experiences from home or play to the workplace, institution or school; bridging from outside school into the classroom at the start of the lesson. This can give a reason for what is to be learned.

Bridging is about making connections

Teachers who help pupils to make connections between concepts are helping them to become more fluent, more able to use their knowledge, more likely to extend their own thinking, more confident to look for new connections and to derive new ideas. Isolated facts at the end of a single track are less likely to be easy to access in a variety of ways and different situations than a fact that is linked to a rich network of paths.

Strategies for differentiation

'Differentiation is a planned process of intervention in the classroom to maximise potential based on individual needs.'   Dickinson C. and Wright J., 1993

Sound differentiation starts with finding out where your pupils are in their learning and attainment. It continues with regular dialogue between teacher and learner concerning the learners' progress and their needs. Differentiation can be by task, resource, support, outcome and response. Differentiation is not only hard to accomplish but means different things to different teachers. Even the terms task, resource, support, outcome and response have been given different meanings. What follows is my own interpretation.

Differentiation by task

Pupils benefit from being told what they are meant to be achieving at the start of a lesson, what is expected of them and what constitutes a good outcome. Give them the 'big picture' if you can. Here strategies vary greatly. Some teachers set different tasks for each group, others offer choice, some match to ability, others match to learning preferences but rarely to interest. I often set a core task with an easier and more advanced variant. I use material with the same content but written at five different levels. Pupils start where they like, based on my recommendation. The challenge is to push them forward rather than let them gravitate to doing the minimum amount of work to get by.

Differentiation by resource

I like to give the same instruction for a task but offer very different resources to complete it with. This results in very different outcomes. These can then be discussed and the nature of the resource explored. Draw or paint a cut-up fruit. Use charcoal, chalk and black paper, pencil, crayon, watercolour, or oil pastel. What happens when squares overlap? Select pinboard and coloured elastic bands, pegboard with coloured pegs, templates to draw round and in, squares of coloured plastic gel and an OHP, gummed paper squares, squares of tissue paper or foam squares and an inkpad. Review outcomes and which resource highlights a particular aspect of the task.

Differentiation by support

This could be from their peers, or from you or other adults in the classroom, for example a classroom or special needs support assistant. Support can be enhanced by co-operative or team teaching and small group tutoring. You could plan extra time to support a particular group or individual. Parents can become involved in supporting their children's work.

Differentiation by outcome

Give the same problem to a group, and if they work on it separately you will end up with different solutions, different strategies employed, and different ways of reporting their findings. This is differentiation by outcome. It will be more likely with open tasks such as investigations. You can encourage it by asking for preferred ways of responding, including written, dramatised, graphical, mimed, or sung to music. You can encourage a creative, risk-taking culture in your classroom or explain that on some occasions a more restrained response is required. A sense of audience is a vital ingredient to ensure an appropriate outcome.

Differentiation by response

This can mean the pupils' response to the task; the product, normally called the outcome. I am particularly interested in the point at which the pupil engages or fails to engage with the task. For me, that is a response to the task. It also can mean the teacher's response to the pupil and/or the pupil's work. This can be verbal or written feedback, intervention during the completion of the task, celebrating the pupil's achievement publicly, suggesting the next step or providing the next task or a modified or different task. As a result of both types of response, the pupil could:

- write in a learning log or booklet which goes home and could contain parents' and teachers' comments as well;

- produce an action plan negotiated with or without the teacher, which contains targets to be achieved;

- arrange one-to-one conferences between peers (response partners) or with an adult.

I used to arrange 20-minute consultations with every member of my class about six weeks into the year. We made the time and they valued the opportunity for a prolonged dialogue. Incidentally, they had to learn to work quietly without my help during these sessions. Could you use this strategy with your pupils? With your induction tutor, consider how you can use your increasing knowledge of your pupils to differentiate work appropriately.

Chapter 7

THE APPLIANCE OF NEUROSCIENCE: THE NEW '-OLOGY'

'John Dewey began this century with an eloquent plea for the education of the whole child. It would be good for us to get around to it by the end of the century.'

Sylwester R., 1995

Chapter contents:

■ **Why bother with Neuroscience as a teacher?**

■ **The Triune Brain**

■ **Emotional intelligence**

■ **Using memory to improve teaching and learning**

■ **Using the senses**

■ **Neuro-Linguistic Programming**

■ **Visual, Auditory and Kinaesthetic**

■ **Forms of communication**

Why bother with Neuroscience as a teacher?

Understanding how the brain works may help us to understand how to make schoolwork more memorable for our pupils. Our brains are designed for survival, not for formal learning. When we are threatened, the blood supply to our neo-cortex and limbic system is reduced and the supply to our old reptilian brain is increased. 'Fight or flight' takes over from engaging in meaningful dialogue based on reasoned argument. When our hackles rise, we behave like chickens, geese, cats or dogs. The same applies when we are forced into submission or humiliated. But when we are stroked, patted, fed and watered, cared for and looked after who knows what we might achieve? (See Smith A., 1996)

Over 80 per cent of our knowledge about the human brain and how it learns has been acquired since the early 1980s. Using modern scanning techniques, such as functional Magnetic Resonance Imaging (fMRI), the brain can be seen in action in 3D, almost in real time. This means that the painstaking data collected from probing the brain with tiny electrodes which might have taken 20 years in the 1960s and 1970s can now be collected in a minute or less with little or no invasion. The impact this is already having on our knowledge is hard to imagine. As yet, few if any teachers have access to the findings of this research and even fewer are confirming or changing what they do in the classroom as a result. Many of the findings confirm what some research projects on teaching and learning have already illuminated, for example:

- the importance of the learner and the teacher being healthy and happy or at least in a non-threatening environment;
- the value of a positive atmosphere of valuing individual effort and raising self-esteem;
- the improved learning through a state of relaxed alertness; high challenge and low stress;
- the significance of narrative and metaphor in teaching;
- the learner's involvement in whole, meaningful challenges;
- the power of presenting material in a variety of ways, using a variety of stimuli such as visual, auditory and kinaesthetic;
- the necessity of providing the learner with an overview, the big picture, a route map or plan of the work;
- the links between mind mapping and concept mapping, and the way our brains hold and link information in a very personal manner;
- the idea that intellect is modifiable;
- the belief that each individual must find their own solutions to problems such as learning to grasp and learning to walk; so why not learning to perform mental arithmetic, to manipulate shapes in your mind and to estimate measurements?

For further detail on this, see the work of Sylwester R., (1995), Smith A., (1996) and Carter R., (1998).

The Triune Brain

The 'Reptilian' Brain: Brainstem and Cerebellum

Herd behaviour in classroom is often like 'reptilian' behaviour, the way you would expect the most primitive part of our brain to react. Look at the behaviours typically associated with the reptilian brain. We need to recognise it as such, treat is as such and get on with helping the class learn how to learn. When we are stressed, blood flow to our reptilian brain is prioritised and our higher thinking almost shuts down. In other words, we are incapable of learning and serious thinking when we are upset. Behaviourism seems to me to deal well with this (see Chapter 4). Without order and a good working atmosphere in your classroom, you will not get to use even the best lesson plans or most exciting activities to create a learning environment.

The 'Mammalian' Brain: the Limbic System

Watching my granddaughter play reminds me that many young children behave as if they have read the work of Jean Piaget. They are not yet fully integrated social beings and their play is imitative, creative, persistent, very physical and often egocentric. You can see that they are emotional beings who are trying to adapt to their environment. Some early parts of this Constructivist view seem to very crudely accord with the interaction between sensory and motor parts of the Cortex and the Limbic System, the 'mammalian' brain which is very powerful and influential in the management and control of information. There are more neural pathways rising from the Limbic System to the higher more advanced parts of the brain than return to it. This means that it always adds an emotional dimension to anything, both before and after it validates what we learn.

Neo-cortex (thinking cap)

Problem solving

Finding relationships

Pattern matching

Pattern making

Generates meaning from sensory data

Limbic System (mid-brain) 'Mammalian'

Holds all three parts in balance, but emotions dominate

Processes and manages information; always with feelings!

Filters valuable data in, filters useless data out

Governs concepts of value and truth

Goal setting: dream with a time-scale

The site of powerful positive and negative emotions

The site of long term memory; we remember experiences with strong emotional associations

Immune system control

Eating, sleeping and sexual patterns

Brain Stem and Cerebellum 'Reptilian'

Survival: fight or flight; screaming; lashing out

Monitoring motor functions: breathing; balance.

Territoriality: defend personal space; possessions and friends

Mating rituals: showing off; attention seeking; preening

Group hierarchies: adhere to place in pecking order

Rote behaviours: repetitive; predictable but rarely constructive (rocking, scratching, head banging)

Paul MacLean (1978)

The 'Human' (or 'Primate') Brain: the Cortex and Neo-cortex

The currently popular and dominant Social Constructivist views of Vygostsky, Bruner and Feuerstein match our ideas about the workings of the 'Primate' outer cortex and neo-cortex of the brain, especially the frontal lobes, responsible for our higher order thinking, and social awareness, amongst others. MacLean's Triune Brain theory leads me to think that we should accept each of these three great psychological theories of this century and consider what part each can play in helping us to help children to learn how to learn.

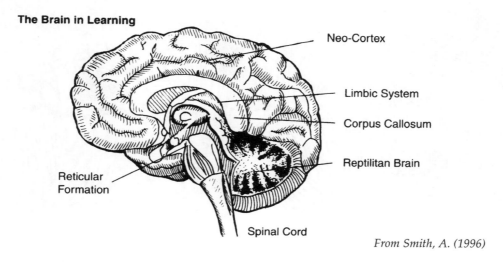

The Brain in Learning

From Smith, A. (1996)

Emotional intelligence

'Our profession pays lip service to educating the whole student, but school activities tend to focus on the development of measurable, rational qualities. We measure students' spelling accuracy but not their emotional well being. And when the budget gets tight, we cut the difficult-to-measure curricular areas, such as the arts, that tilt towards emotion.'

Sylwester R. (1995)

Emotions are the glue that could help us to make an integrated curriculum out of a curriculum composed of separate, logically defined disciplines:

Developing emotional intelligence	Classroom strategies
Accepting and controlling our emotions	Circle time, singing, dancing, painting, playing games
Using meta-cognitive activities	Talking about and listening to people's feelings, asking why?
Using activities that promote social interaction	Drama, role-play, games, discussions, field trips, co-operative learning
Using activities that provide emotional context	Simulations, role-play, drama, co-operative projects
Avoiding emotional stress	Promoting self-esteem and control over own environment, making own rules, circle time
Recognise the relationship between emotions and health	Ensuring that the classroom is a stimulating, emotionally positive, warm and safe place to be

Using memory to improve teaching and learning

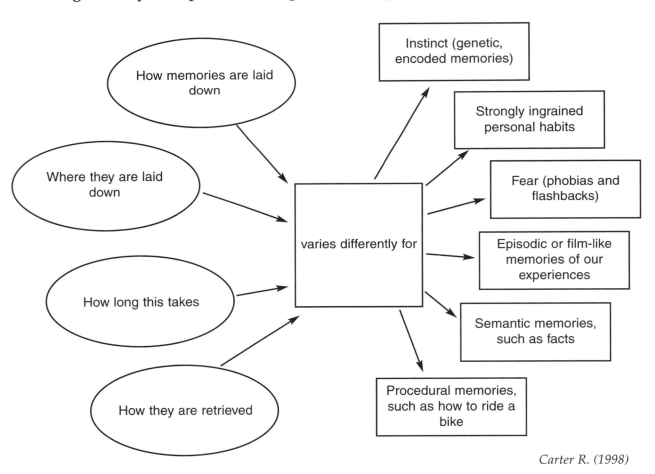

How memories are laid down

Where they are laid down

How long this takes

How they are retrieved

varies differently for

Instinct (genetic, encoded memories)

Strongly ingrained personal habits

Fear (phobias and flashbacks)

Episodic or film-like memories of our experiences

Semantic memories, such as facts

Procedural memories, such as how to ride a bike

Carter R. (1998)

If children come to school to learn and to learn how to learn, then working on how to make things memorable and easy to remember must surely be one important aspect of learning for both teacher and pupil. Even though our understanding of memory has advanced in recent years, it is still incomplete. We know however that when powerful long-term memories return, they are often involved with a full range of sensations such as colour, sound, smell and touch. We all know that certain smells very quickly produce positive or negative memories. Our brains are designed for survival and it is really important to remember events which were life threatening or highly beneficial. I doubt we can fill every school day with the positive kind but I hope that we can avoid introducing powerful negative memories which might reduce self-esteem and act as a block to learning.

How can knowledge about how memory works help us to improve both teaching and learning? In the following sections are some simple suggestions.

Using the senses

Use as many of the five or more senses as you can sensibly and safely. Use the senses as a checklist. Handling historical or old objects such as Greek coins from 500BC or your great granny's handbag from 1923 can be a memorable experience for a child or adult, especially if a story is woven around it. Looking at, drawing and handling animals, be they gerbils, mini-beasts under magnification, sea creatures in a clear plastic jar or a 6m python skin can be unforgettable. Put everyday objects in a 'feelie' bag or empty crisp box. Get young children to describe what they can feel. Can they put together puzzles by touch alone? How can we introduce sound? Can we make use of music, noises, birdsong and transposed elephant or whale sounds? Why do we so rarely use smell and taste in our teaching? How can we do it safely? I've often asked pupils to draw, sketch, cut up, redraw, taste and cook with unusual ingredients. The Aztecs used avocado, chilli, maize, peppers and chocolate. The children's artwork in pencil and pastel crayons was only surpassed by their tortillas, chilli dip, guacamole and chocolatl. Try to make one lesson each week a bit more sensual in some way. Think about how you might stimulate one particular sense. Then watch to see which children respond dramatically.

Neuro-Linguistic Programming (NLP)

Neuro-Linguistic Programming came out of the search for excellence in various therapies and trying to determine what makes a professional expert.

Neuro: The neurological processes of hearing, seeing, feeling, tasting and smelling are the basic building blocks of our experience.
Linguistic: The ways in which we use language to represent our experience and communicate with others.
Programming: The strategies that we use to organise these inner processes to produce results.

We construct our own internal model of the world, based on our perceptions. For us, it is the real world, the world as we know it. Most human problems derive from the problems in our heads rather than from the world as it really is. By developing meta-knowledge about our own inner models, we can change our habits, thoughts and feelings from unhelpful into helpful.

Some major pre-suppositions of Neuro-Linguistic Programming

"Contentment is not the fulfilment of what you want, but the realisation of how much you already have."   (See NLP web site in Bibliography)

If we pre-suppose the following statements to be true and act as if they were, then we might find our lives and their many interactions with others become more flexible, creative, positive and enriched.

Just about anyone can learn to do anything. If one person can do something, it should be possible to model it and teach it to someone else.

We are all responsible for creating our own experience. Typically, we have much more control than we think we have.

The mind and body are one system. A change in one affects the other. They mutually influence one another.

If you want to understand, then act. You will learn through doing.

If what you are doing is not working, then do something else. It is not wrong to make a second choice.

We have all the resources that we need. There are no unresourceful people, only unresourceful states. We need to learn how to access these more resourceful states, at the right time and place.

People work perfectly. No one is wrong or broken; it is a matter of finding out how they function now, so that you can help them to change to a more useful or desirable state.

There is no such thing as failure, only feedback. Try to use every response.

Human behaviour is purposeful; even though we are not always conscious of that purpose. Find out what people's reasons are for what they do.

All behaviour has a positive intention. A person is not their behaviour. We can separate the action from the purpose behind the action. Ask this question of the action: "What is the positive intention of this action?" Listen for the reply and note it.

The meaning of the communication is the response you get. All communication provokes response and feedback. It may not be what we hoped for, but we can still use it usefully to improve communication.

We are always communicating. There are five representational systems: Visual, Auditory, Kinaesthetic, Olfactory and Gustatory.

Having a choice is better than not having a choice. Try to act to increase choice. The person with the greatest number of choices and the greatest flexibility of thought and behaviour has the greatest influence in an interaction. The person with the most flexibility controls the system.

The map is not the territory. People respond to their map of reality, not to reality itself. NLP is the science of changing these maps, not trying to change reality.

Visual, Auditory and Kinaesthetic (VAK)

Over many years, you tend to develop intuitive awareness about people's needs. You watch and listen to every aspect of their persona. Faced with 30 children at the start of your teaching career, this may seem a little unrealistic. If you can calm yourself and train yourself to be still, opening yourself up to children's dominant ways of taking in ideas, thinking about them and expressing themselves, then you will notice:

- which children stare out of the window, love watching nature, are entranced by patterns and colour, doodle when you are talking to them and crave art. Try to encourage and develop their strengths (Visual);

- which children love to hear stories, real, imagined or read. They can become authors, scriptwriters and actors with your help (Auditory);

- which children have to touch and fiddle with objects, toys, their hair, clothes and can't wait for PE or games. Can you make their learning as active as possible? Try to help them to develop fine motor co-ordination (Kinaesthetic):

Language used by children and adults can also give you clues to their preferences. Listen out for words associated with Visual, Auditory or Kinaesthetic.

"I see your point of view."
Visual   see, watch, view, observe, looks, reveals, perspective, focus, picture

"I hear what you say and that sounds fine to me."
Auditory   hear, tell, say, ask, sounds, listen, speak

"That idea doesn't feel right, it doesn't grab me."
Kinaesthetic   move, hit, touch, feel, struggle, grab, do, go with that, struck by the idea, act out

The VAK analysis leaves out taste and smell, but these can be observed in children's preferences, in the way they say and do things and in the way they respond to and are obviously influenced by your own preferences. Firstly, find out more about yourself, then look for what others seem to need. Try to ensure that your lessons have all three elements in some form or other.

Think about the three phases of the lesson: INPUT, PROCESS, OUTPUT. If each phase has opportunities for V, A and K, then you optimise the chances of all the learners engaging, working on and being able to respond to the task. Often, it is unrealistic to plan for all three modes in all three phases of the lesson. Differentiation by resources and differentiation by response may make more sense to you now. Choose one topic or concept that you want to teach and consider how you can make it more sensual and more accessible to more of the pupils you teach. Will they be allowed to respond in different ways or must it always be written or spoken? Could it be a drawing, diagram or mime? Think how useful and important dance, PE and especially drama can be in allowing many of those you teach the maximum number of opportunities to engage with, work on, make sense of, learn from and remember.

Realise how important:

- demonstrating and modelling are to those who like to watch;

- reading, explaining and discussing are for those who like to hear or listen.

Think about how frustrated the others will be when waiting to get their hands on the material.

Use a variety of resources to act as a stimulus, not just the ones which might stimulate you. Vary your own input, sometimes say nothing, just demonstrate, ask for explanation; at other times get the 'doers' to show the rest of the class. This feels natural in PE, dance, drama and art, so why not other subjects? Make the VAK model open in your planning and teaching; tell pupils what you are doing and why. Ask for feedback, advice and suggestions. Identify pupils' preferences and strengths, lead with these strengths, develop them, then help them to develop their needs. So as you as a teacher become aware of your own preferences, use and develop them, turn them to the other areas. In so doing, you expose the pupils to other forms of your input. Ideally, you and they need to be able to work with V, A and K in all three stages. Alistair Smith (1998) suggests many practical ways of using VAK in the classroom, for example in approaches to teaching spelling.

Forms of communication

Written	Auditory/spoken	Graphical	Visual	Other forms
Algebra	Ceremonies	Annotate sketch	2D and 3D models	Ballet
Book review	Conversation	Computer print out	Advertisement	Braille
Diary	Debate	Concept map	Body language	Dance
Letter/e-mail	Interview	Design	Cartoon	Movement
List	Jokes	Diagram	Colour-coding	Multi-media
Newspaper	Morse code	Drawing	Computer	Music
Notes	Play	Flow chart	Exhibition	Recorded music
Numbers	Poem	Graphs	Logos	Scent
Play-script	Prayer	Maps	Mime	Smells
Poem	Radio programme	Mind map	Photograph	Song
Questionnaire	Rhythms	Plan	Puppets	Thinking
Recipe	Role play	Sketches	Sign language	Touch
Report	Tape conversation	Spider diagram	Signs	Virtual reality
Story	Telephone call	Time-line	Video	Written music

This list shows how you can broaden choices for the way we communicate, how we give out and take in information; especially the ways in which children respond to tasks.

INPUT: How do you like to receive information?

PROCESS: How do you like to process information?

OUTPUT: How do you like to output information?

Are we all the same? Are the forms of communication the same for all three stages? What should we offer children? What would you add, move or remove? Are all the entries of the same order or are some sub-sets of others?

Two practical examples of using VAK techniques are shown below. Use the forms of communication checklist to develop VAK in all phases of your lessons. What would be appropriate in each phase? Pick out the communication forms that interest you and put them into a grid similar to those below, choosing your own teaching topic or unit of work, and using the two completed examples as a guide. Try teaching the lesson that you have planned. Discuss it with your induction tutor.

A story about 'Lost Sheep'	Visual	Auditory	Kinaesthetic
Input **Take in**	Models of sheep on hills.	Narrative and explanation.	Movement of the shepherd and dog.
Process **Think about**	Contours and map. Can shepherd see sheep?	Discussion of finding the sheep.	Looking and moving figures on the model.
Output **Response**	Draw a cross-section of hills. Write what you found out.	Explain findings to class. Say what you have learnt.	Stretch a length of coloured wool from sheep to shepherd and dog.

Teaching Kinetic Molecular Theory	Visual	Auditory	Kinaesthetic
Input **Take in**	Demonstrate model with polystyrene balls in a box.	Hear sound of movement. Explain.	Role-play solid to liquid to gas.
Process **Think about**		Say what you see. Discuss.	
Output **Response**	Watch others. Draw pictures of solid, liquid and gas.	Predict solid, liquid or gas.	Demonstrate solid, liquid and gas with bodies.

Chapter 8

LEARNING STYLES, TEACHING STYLES AND CLASSROOM ORGANISATION

It is important that, as NQTs, you see yourselves as professionals right from the beginning. Monitor your own teaching for a balance of approaches but don't try out too many new ideas at the same time.

Induction tutor

Chapter contents:

- **Using educational theory to develop your teaching**

- **Using Gardner's Eight Kinds of Learning Style in the classroom**

- **Connecting Left brain and Right brain: 'Practice makes perfect'**

- **Instrumental Enrichment and Mediated Learning**

- **Unusual activities and surprises**

Using educational theory to develop your teaching

We need to provide our children with a love of learning so that they are willing and eager to embark on lifelong learning. Most babies are born with more than enough curiosity to sustain this desire to learn, but somehow we stifle it. To avoid this, they should learn how to learn. It should not be a well kept secret or mystery. All too often, thinking skills and problem-solving strategies are seen as irrelevant or an optional extra.

Pupils must to be able to solve problems and investigate serious questions for themselves and be able to work as part of a team. They need to become autonomous problem solvers and good collaborators. They will require increasingly sophisticated levels of literacy, numeracy, graphicacy and information-handling skills for this and to be able to cope with the Internet.

They need to develop an informed world view with an understanding of other cultures. They should be able to speak other languages fluently. They need to acquire a set of values that allows them to make informed moral and rational decisions and choices.

Much media attention has been given to the 'traditional versus progressive' debate. Is it relevant? Democratic classrooms which form an essential part of programmes such as Highscope (which involves circle time), Philosophy for Children, Instrumental Enrichment, Lateral Thinking and other thinking skills initiatives stress the importance of giving children choices, time to plan and time to think, valuing what children bring and what they know, encouraging children to share their ideas and views, evaluate and criticise their own work, and genuinely feel that they have a say. (See Fisher, 1990, and Claxton, 1990)

It seems to me that all these thinking programmes and some educational innovations have certain factors in common:

- the need for the individual to find out who they are;

- the raising of self-esteem;

- the need to be listened to and to have a fair hearing;

- the need to listen to and question others;

- no need to use an outside authority;

- they are structured by material or procedure;

- they have an open agenda;

- they start with the learner's questions and concerns.

Atkinson (1992) and Lewis (1996) put forward ideas that you, as the teacher, could use in response:

- help the class to devise a set of classroom rules;

- negotiate and explain the pattern of work for the day, week or term;

- negotiate and plan topics with and for the class, group or individual;

- encourage the class to gather resources and information;

- demonstrate or model a new activity;

- work with a group leading and sharing in an activity;

- act as facilitator by taking notes, recording votes, seeing fair play;

- encourage children to take on a variety of roles;

- help individuals to set up targets, make contracts or monitor independent activity.

There is mounting evidence (see Askew 1995) that using a variety of teaching strategies develops and encourages autonomous problem solvers, prepared to work with others and share their ideas as part of a multi-disciplinary team that includes very different people with different abilities. What do children know when they come to school and can they show it? (See Hughes, 1986, and Pound, 1999.) Most children know, but cannot necessarily show you that they know, an extensive amount about their daily lives. They may well find it hard to transfer this knowledge into a new setting or context such as school.

There is much educational theory that can help you to develop your teaching style. You may not want to explore them all; indeed you may not have the time. You may not agree with them all. But they are worth considering. I have taken as starting points:

- Gardner's Eight Intelligences (1983);

- Hemispherical Specialisation: Left Brain/Right Brain (McCarthy, 1983);

- Mediated Learning and Instrumental Enrichment (Feuerstein, 1983).

I believe that these frameworks will help you to discover:

- the range of abilities shown by children and their different approaches to learning;

- the variety of opportunities for activity and the range of materials on offer;

- the need to plan across the curriculum and organise time and resources.

Use these materials, the resources you will gather and make and the expertise of the other teachers you work with to:

- try to find out what children know and can do and help them to develop these strengths;

- provide a variety of learning opportunities which will engage and challenge children;

- plan a broad and balanced curriculum.

Using Gardner's Eight Kinds of Learning Style in the classroom

Children who are strongly:	think:	enjoy:	need:	follow instructions such as:
Linguistic	in words	reading, writing, telling stories, playing word games	books, tapes, writing tools, paper, diaries, discussion, debate, stories	read about, write about, talk about, listen to
Logical-Mathematical	by reasoning	experimenting, questioning, calculating, puzzles, logic games	things to explore and puzzle over, science materials, museums	quantify, think critically about, conceptualise
Spatial	in images and pictures	drawing, designing, making, visualising, doodling	art, moving images, illustrated books, construction materials, galleries	see, draw, make, visualise, colour, map
Bodily-Kinaesthetic	through body sensations	dancing, running, jumping, climbing, building, touching, gesturing	movement, role-play, drama, building materials, sports, physical games, tactile materials	build, act out, touch, dance
Musical	via rhythms and melodies	singing, whistling, humming, tapping feet and hands, listening	sing-along time, records, tapes, playing musical instruments, concerts	sing, play, rap, beat out, listen to
Interpersonal	by bouncing ideas off others	leading, organising, manipulating, mediating, partying	social gatherings, group games, clubs, friends, apprenticeship	collaborate, teach, interact with, share
Intrapersonal	deeply inside themselves	setting goals, mediating, dreaming, being quiet, planning	time alone, secret places, self-paced projects	connect it to your personal life, dream about it, plan
Naturalist	about their environment	working in nature, exploring and learning about plants and animals, feeling a part of the world, being outdoors	to be in nature, opportunities to observe and identify flora and fauna, interdependence, life cycles and bio-rhythms	classify, observe, link structure and function, look for rhythm/cycles, describe the whole

Think about these types of children. What teaching activities would best suit each learning style? Which would be the most appropriate learning resources to support the activities?

Connecting Left brain and Right brain: 'Practice makes perfect'

We need to develop automaticity, like fluency in reading, the ability to do things without thinking and worrying about them, for example number bonds, facts, tables, musical scales, arpeggios, words, handwriting, brush strokes, and dance steps, but in meaningful contexts. Making links between things we know about already and new ideas is one of the most powerful ways of connecting and holding on to those new ideas. If we find the connections for ourselves, given time, space and encouragement, then the links are more relevant to us. Often, concepts taught in school have a ready-made conceptual structure with predetermined links thought out by a good and thorough teacher, but sometimes what we learn at school is of no use elsewhere or perhaps we cannot connect it up. There is little transfer to other areas and no real application that might keep it alive. The concept of bridging is dealt with in Chapter 6. This concerns how to make work relevant and connected. There is, I believe, great potential for bridging in numeracy and literacy work.

One of the best ways to ensure connections is to try to use both halves of your brain, both left and right hemispheres. Use the lists below to assess yourself. Are you left dominant, right dominant or fairly balanced? Remember that this is just another model and not an absolute 'truth'. Use it if you find it helpful. We want to 'work from strength' and help children to develop what they can already do. We also want them to become as balanced as possible. We need both hemispheres to work effectively.

Some characteristics of Hemispherical Specialisation (McCarthy B., 1983)

Left Mode	Right Mode
Rational	Intuitive
Verbal	Visuo-spatial
Logical	Analogical
Analytical, showing detail	Integrative, showing structure
Linear	Parallel
Sequential	Simultaneous
Objective	Subjective
Controlled systematic experiments	Open-ended random experiments
Problem-solves by logically and sequentially looking at the parts of things	Problem-solves by hunching, looking for patterns and configurations
Responds to verbal instructions	Responds to demonstrated instructions
Looks at differences	Looks at similarities
Is planned and structured	Is fluid and spontaneous
Prefers established, certain information	Prefers elusive, uncertain information
Analyses	Synthesises
Primary reliance on language in thinking and remembering	Primary reliance on images in thinking and remembering
Prefers talking and writing	Prefers drawing and manipulating
Responsive to structure	Responsive to ambience
Prefers hierarchical authority	Prefers collegial authority
Sees cause and effect	Sees correspondence
Is theoretical	Is experiential
More sensitive to verbal sounds	More sensitive to natural sounds
Excels in propositional language	Excels in poetic, metaphoric language

Superior in:	*Superior in:*
Writing	Drawing
Digit and letter recognition	Verbal imagery
Naming shapes	Non-verbal dimensions; depth, tone, hue
Word recognition	Photos, schematic figures
Phonic discriminations	Tactile discriminations
Slower, serial, analytic difference detection	Rapid, global, identity matching
Drawing on previously accumulated, organised information	Drawing on unbounded, non-sequential, qualitative patterns linked to felt images

Mind mapping and concept mapping are two right-brain dominant techniques that you might find personally useful and want to use with your pupils. (See Buzan T., 1991, and Novak J. and Gowin V., 1984.)

There are numerous major links between different parts of the brain. It is a distributed network, with modules of the brain performing specific tasks when ordered to do so and passing the resulting information to other areas. There are usually a number of different ways of getting from one module to another. Some of the routes are very fast but 'dirty', (where little or no conscious thought has been applied); others are more circuitous. Often, the Limbic system (the Mammalian part of our brain; see Chapter 7) will mediate and control the passing of information. We could never cope if we were conscious of all the information coming in, being processed and going out. In an emergency, we get ready to act without thinking and we have no initial conscious control over where the information is sent. A fast 'dirty' route makes us prepare to act whilst consciously we are mulling over the information to decide if there is a real threat or not. Normally, we can pull back or press on. Often, we use our conscious mind to rationalise what our subconscious has already decided for us. We probably do not have as much free will as we think we have (See Claxton G., 1998).

All of our thoughts are coloured and influenced to a greater or lesser extent by the Limbic system. However cool we think we are being, all of our thoughts have an emotional component and are soaked in values which we hold deeply. Our most profound intellectual achievements and ideas are the product of a value set rooted in our deepest emotions (See Goleman D., 1996). It is ridiculous to try to define intelligence as any one thing. We now have many theories and ideas, most of which allude to or try to define a host of brain modules each working away to solve particular parts of a problem and working in consort to produce a solution.

Instrumental Enrichment and Mediated Learning

'Mediate as little as possible, but as much as necessary.'

Reuven Feuerstein

It is vital to fire up these brain modules, to get them working and encourage them to interact with other brain modules. The best examples of firing up and wiring up modules that I know of are to be found in the work of Reuven Feuerstein, and in the Somerset Thinking Skills Course (Blagg *et al.*, 1988) based on Feuerstein's work. Feuerstein, who worked with Jean Piaget, believes that specific cognitive skills can and should be taught. They can be linked and bridged to everyday situations. In short, we can teach children to think and solve problems. He is not alone in the belief that helping children to 'learn how to learn' is essential if they are to reach their full potential as individuals whatever their disabilities. Furthermore, whole schools, areas and countries should be able to improve their education systems, producing individuals who can better cope with life and at least try to solve whatever problems are thrown at them.

He views the role of the parent, teacher or other significant adult as essential in the mediation of the learning experience. It is not enough in his view to surround the child with exciting stimuli, fascinating experiences and wondrous opportunities. In fact, the child may remain cognitively deprived if there is no significant adult to mediate these experiences for the learner. Mediation entails relating and linking disparate aspects of the experience in order that the child can build up a coherent model of the world. This is done by explaining, emphasising, interpreting and extending both the cultural and local significance of the experience and also the wider and more universal implications. I remember being four years old and stamping on a slug. My father explained very carefully all the aspects of what I had just done. The slug was dead and I had taken its life. It had ceased to exist as a living thing. I don't think I realised that it would die or what death really meant. What would happen if I continued to stamp on and kill anything that I didn't like the look or feel of, asked my father? What would the world be like if everyone behaved like me? I was surprised that he was upset by my behaviour, but I listened carefully, staring at the stain on the path, not wishing to displease him further. I can remember the incident very clearly still. It was a milestone in building my understanding of the world.

Even children with sensory deficits or emotional problems can in Feuerstein's experience fulfil their potential, as he has demonstrated so many times since 1945, when he started working in Israel with orphans who had survived the Holocaust, many of whom had worked as children in the concentration camps. I believe that the following factors have led to his impressive results over the past 50 years:

- a combination of his detailed diagnostic techniques to pinpoint what a child can and cannot do: the Learning Potential Acquisition Device (LPAD);

- the careful structuring of his remedial materials for Instrumental Enrichment, where the emphasis is on thinking process rather than knowledge acquisition;

- the insistent nature of his work with children, giving them time to complete the tasks, then discuss them and bridge what has been learnt to other situations and everyday life;

- the fact that the brain can sometimes find another route if the normal one is blocked or damaged.

Feuerstein's results demonstrate the enormous plasticity and modifiability of the human intellect, and the importance of the role played by significant adults in the child's mental growth. IQ tests measure what has been learned in some specific and restricted areas. They do not measure what can be learned, or all the areas in which learning can take place. They certainly do not predict capacity for learning. There has been a move towards more interactive teaching, active learning, problem-solving and investigative approaches and the adopting of a range of strategies in some subjects. This is one reason that I keep repeating the suggestion of encouraging children to respond in a variety of ways. I remember Peter and Shaun, two nine-year-olds who could barely write. I suggested that they scribbled, drew or made marks for their answers to a comprehension test. I had been reading Aesop's fables to the class at the start of a new school year. I read two different fables before morning break and I was asking the questions after break; sneaky, but designed to help them improve their memories. When we came to mark the work, both Peter and Shaun were perfectly able to identify marks on the paper, which they marked right or wrong. To me they meant nothing. This was a critical incident for me. I started using De Bono's drawing techniques such as re-designing a chocolate-making machine, a dog-exercising machine or an elephant-weighing machine. Over the next few months, their ability to draw diagrams, annotate and explain them became impressive. Shaun and Peter really started to communicate.

Feuerstein's Learning Potential Acquisition Device is designed to find out what the child can and cannot do; which channels are open, which are closed, which phases operate and which are stuck. It is our job, as teachers, to use this information to help our pupils to learn in whichever style suits them best. In the next part of the chapter, I suggest some practical examples of activities, which you could consider using in your classroom.

Unusual activities and surprises

The more interested we are, the more likely an event is to persist in our memory. At night, we recycle the events of the day. Some thoughts 'stay with us'. Sometimes we awake with the solution to a problem. When I shave in the morning is often my most creative time as the thoughts that my sleep has brought me surface into my consciousness.

We all like nice surprises. School needs routines but these can become too predictable and boring. One way to gain a class's attention is to surprise them at the start of the session, by including a joke, a bit of magic, dressing up, pretending to be asleep or even awake perhaps, cycling into the classroom and using the bike for work on gears, ratio, friction or bearings, producing and using a puppet or playing a game. It is better if your opening gambit has some relevance to the work to be done. Doing something surprising once a term should enhance your reputation and you might enjoy the risk taking, surprise yourself and try it more often!

Here are some of my surprises:

Pass around some unknown object and ask for their comments, suggestions and anything they recognise about it. Examples include a fossil, old coin, whale vertebrae, Victorian children's marble, Russian doll, sea urchin/starfish, old miniature painting, gas mask, clutch cable, carving, snuff box, dodecahedron, crystal, a pottery fragment, strange dried fruit, flower, plant or leaf.

Reveal object(s) one at a time from inside a suitcase, an old bag or under a cloth. I've used objects from the list above and a 6m python skin, wind surfing sail, old letters and documents from my family and other sources, old newspapers, books and magazines, unusual fruit or vegetables, and a collection of tin whistles and flutes.

You could ask them to guess what is in the bag. Sometimes, wrapping the object up like a present and playing pass the parcel works well. Get one pupil to write down all the questions that are asked about the object as it is passed around, clearly and in order. Give no answers, just collect questions. Then discuss how we might find answers. Where could we look? Who could we ask? What observations, measurements, investigations, might we be able to conduct? Starting from their questions about an object or set of objects you have collected gives you some control of direction and content but demands their interests.

You might ask them to bring objects in. Be very wary of old hand grenades, bombs and shells. It has been known for unexploded munitions to be brought into classrooms. If this happens call the Bomb Disposal Unit!

Anything unusual may help to stimulate the start of a topic of a series of lessons. A new face, a visitor to talk about their life, work or interests. A visit to a local park, shop or factory. I often advise NQTs to wander around the local area of their new school at the weekend. Go to the local shops, look for the local park and interesting buildings and don't forget to look at the potential offered by the school grounds. For example, one primary school in the centre of Plymouth has developed a marvellous range of areas over a period of more than 10 years, including a butterfly garden, herb garden, different brick, stone and paving patterns, small tree collection, fossil and rock trail, mini beast area, recycling area, and board games from around the world professionally made to playground scale. These facilities can be used in and out of lesson time.

I like to set the occasional 'trap' for children to fall into. This might be in the form of a Giant's footprints on the ceiling, or a tiny handprint on a windowpane when they come into the room. I say nothing. Work on scale and measurement results. I might read a passage or show a video from *The Borrowers*. What would it be like to be so small or so large? Interview a giant or a tiny person. One of the pupils pretends to be the giant or tiny person. What questions would you ask them? Make an artefact for a tiny person. Collect everyday objects and ask them how the tiny person might use them, for example cotton thread, needle, pin, nail, lollipop stick, plastic dustbin bag, and a plastic cup.

Try developing a 'Skills Register', where pupils and adults can share their expertise. Find out what pupils' friends, parents and relatives can do. Invite them into your classroom. A parent working on cantilever bridge design, explaining forces, tension and compression with carefully made models to a fascinated class sticks in my mind. I also remember a great granny talking to my history class about what the school was like when she was there and and how she worked in the cotton mills for the whole of her adult life.

You will probably find more examples in your school. Ask your induction tutor and other colleagues for ideas. Make your teaching as interesting and memorable as possible.

Chapter 9

UNDERSTANDING OURSELVES AND OTHERS

'When someone knocks on the front door of life, who is going to get there first – the Parent, the Adult or the Child?'

Harris T., 1973

> **Chapter contents:**
>
> ■ **Transactional Analysis: 'I'm OK, you're OK'**
>
> ■ **Using Transactional Analysis to your advantage**
>
> ■ **Using Action Research**

In seeking to understand ourselves and others, especially those we work with and live with, I am suggesting two different approaches:

Transactional Analysis

This gives us insights into ourselves and those we work and live with by helping us to listen, respond to and come to know the Parent, Adult and Child within us all so we may engage in more meaningful dialogue with ourselves and others.

Action Research

This could raise us above the teacher as just a compliant technician who has satisfied a set of standards. Action Research may help us to become autonomous, competent professionals, able to reflect on and act on our working lives in order to make things better for ourselves and for those we work with. Reflective practice can encourage us to know why and to more widely articulate those views based on enquiry and evidence.

Transactional Analysis: 'I'm OK, you're OK'

When your new headteacher addresses you, do you feel like an adult or like a child? What happens if you respond as a child? As a parent? When you talk to children, do you expect an adult response? If you get it, how should you respond? You should strive for an adult to adult interaction unless the children are very young indeed, or the person you are talking to needs 'strokes' (positive comforting actions or words) from you, or you choose to play a different part.

Transactional Analysis can provide you with insight into the different 'parts' that we play in our many and varied relationships at home and at work, in public and with our friends. We play out three 'parts'; those of Parent, Child and Adult. 'I'm OK, you're OK'

---

studies the reaction and interaction between these three parts and often provides a good explanation of when things go wrong in a relationship and how to put it right.

Harris (1973) argues that as infants we all normally end up in a universal **'I'm not OK, you're OK'** position. We feel that our parents are OK but we (quite rightly) cannot have everything that we want when we want it. The aim is to work on understanding our three voices so that we can develop the Adult, make a conscious decision to change and move into an **'I'm OK, you're OK'** position. The other three positions are based on feelings and, once a position is established in early childhood, all experience is selectively interpreted to support it.

The other two positions are:

'I'm not OK, you're not OK': (I'm unloved, never 'stroked') is properly the subject for psychiatrists and psychotherapists or (if the 'stroking' doesn't get through) is possibly Autism.
'I'm OK, you're not OK': an example of this is the battered and physically abused child who only feels OK in the absence of pain, i.e. when they are on their own 'licking their wounds'.
Being able to recognise these positions as a teacher could be important for the children you work with.

<u>P</u>arent, <u>A</u>dult and <u>C</u>hild have a specific meaning in Transactional Analysis. They are not roles, but psychological realities produced by the playback of recorded data of events in the past involving real people, real times, real places, real decisions and real feelings. Past events are recorded in the mind, inextricably linked to our feelings at the time. We probably have locked in our memories most experiences from birth onwards and some from even before birth. This doesn't mean we have conscious access to it all. A stimulus such as a smell, taste, sound or something said can evoke hidden memories so that we experience the feelings associated with that memory without knowing why. (See Penfield W., 1977)

The Parent

This is a huge collection of unedited recordings of unquestioned or imposed external events during a child's pre-school years. For most children, the more significant data from this period will come from experiences with parents and carers. Much of this externally imposed data is concerned with procedures for eating, getting up, getting dressed, blowing your nose, asking politely for things and so on.

Parent clues:

Physical: furrowed brow, pursed lips, pointing finger, head wagging, the 'horrified look' and, for each of you, your own parents' gestures.
Verbal: "How many times have I told you? If I were you … Never, ever let me see you do/say that again. Why do you always…?" 'Never' and 'always' reveal the parent systems that are closed to new data.

The Child

Whilst external events are recorded as the Parent, the simultaneous internal events, the responses of the little person to what they see and hear, are also being recorded. It is this 'seeing, hearing, feeling and understanding' body of data which is defined as the Child. In the early days, the Child has no words with which to construct meaning and so will react with feelings.

Child clues:

Physical: Tears, quivering lip, pouting, temper tantrums, high pitched whiney voice, shrugging shoulders, downcast eyes, teasing, delight, laughter, pulling faces, squirming and giggling.
Verbal: "I wish, I want, I don't want, I don't care, I'm going to, mine's bigger/better/best/ smaller/worst…"

The Adult

Once children begin to crawl, then walk and talk, they can begin to manipulate the world, to choose a response, to direct themselves and move out to meet life. Adult data is beginning to accumulate as a result of their ability to find out what is different about life from the 'taught concept' of life in the Parent and the 'felt concept' of life in the Child. The Adult develops a 'thought concept' of life from their own awareness and original thought. (See Harris T., 1973)

Adult clues:

Physical: Attentive, aware, listening, slight movement of the eyes, face and body. Get any book on body language!
Verbal: "What…, why…, when…, where…, who…, how…, how many…, in what way…? In my opinion…, I think…, I see…, true, false, probable, possible."

Possible interactions between the three voices/parts

Notice how often in life people's behaviour becomes a self-fulfilling prophecy. Treat them like children and they will behave like children. How do you feel if your manager treats you like a five-year-old? How should you respond? Try asserting yourself calmly as an adult and demand to be heard as an adult. Do not get hooked into reacting like a child. Look at the nine possible parallel interactions on the grid.

You \ Them	Adult	Parent	Child
Adult			
Parent			
Child			

This assumes that they respond to the part you are playing. If they do, then you might be able to communicate. A transaction will occur in any parallel interaction, e.g. A to C and C back to A. "How is the book going? " "Oh I don't think I can finish it." "I'm sure you will." "I'm no good at finishing things." "Well dear, you've finished four houses, four children and four jobs." Notice how the Adult (my wife) stays in the Adult part. If, however, your wires are crossed; you want to play Adult to Adult but they want to play Child and provoke a Parent response from you, little or no communication will result, or you will be provoked into playing the part they want you to play. "How is the book going?" "Oh I don't think I can finish it." "Well it's about time you did. Then you can get some of those jobs done that I asked you to do in September." End of transaction. No 'strokes'. Potential hostility.

P to P: Schools aren't what they used to be. No I agree. Back to the basics, I say. You are so right. Well it was good enough for me; we didn't need calculators.

A to A: I'm concerned about 3C's behaviour, but I'm not sure what to do. What precisely are you worried about? A few of them talk too much and are off task. Have you confronted them individually with this? No, that's a good idea, I'll try it, thanks.

C to A: I don't think I can cope with 3C any more. I thought that their behaviour was better when I saw you with them yesterday.

C to P: I don't like doing fractions. If you don't do them, I'll get really cross.
C to A: I don't like doing fractions. Would you like me to help you?
C to C: I don't like doing fractions. I don't like them either, I think they are 'pants'!

(A) Where could I find more A4 paper please? (P) You haven't used it up already, have you? (A) No, I only used about 50 sheets. (P) Well, it doesn't grow on trees. (C) It does!

(A – C) Could you put that chewing gum in the bin please? (P – C) When I'm ready, I'll see. (Feel your hackles rise!) (P – C) No, NOW! (P – C) Not if you shout at me.

(A to A) I must get those reports done tonight. (P to C) You're always leaving things till the last minute.

Using Transactional Analysis to your advantage

'Transactional Analysis is a way of analysing the interactions between two individuals for which the basic unit, the transaction, is composed of a transactional stimulus when one person says or does something, expecting it to be noticed by another who responds in some way, the transactional response.'
Berne E., 1964

You probably recognised many of the examples given above, but here are some typical transactions to help in practical situations:
You using Adult voice: "Could you come and observe me teach this week, please?"
Tutor using Child voice: "Oh, I can't cope. I've so much to do and no-one ever helps me." (pouting, appealing eyes, expecting parental response; a stroke)
You staying as Adult: "I'm sorry to hear that. Is there anything I could do to help so that you could find time to observe me?"
OR
You using Adult voice: "Could you come and observe me teach this week, please?"

Tutor using Parent voice: "Surely I don't have to watch you again. How many times do you expect me to watch you teach Literacy Hour?" (Fed up with demanding child.)
You staying as Adult: "I agree. I can swap my teaching around." (You realise that they are only free on Wednesday mornings)
Tutor gives Adult response: "Good." (Tentative)
You reinforce the Adult: "What would you like to see me teach? PE?" (A submissive offering, which is gratefully accepted.) Transaction successfully completed.

Hopefully, this is an imaginary scenario, but I make the point that an Adult response can result in creative mediation, encouraging the adult and continuing the transaction. Retaliation or playing someone at their own game might not help. We all have bad days and speak without thinking. For you as the NQT, it is all too easy to feel unloved, unwanted, a nuisance, a burden, guilty, wronged, or just plain uncomfortable. By trying to recognise the voice (actor) in yourself, avoiding retaliation, and thinking of an adult response rather than replying with the Child or the Parent in you, much heartache can be avoided. The old adage "Treat them like children and they'll behave like children" has a ring of truth. Can you treat those you teach with respect, give them responsibility, and watch your own language and responses carefully? Can you draw out and educate the Adult in them, rather than regress to the Child in you or bully them with the Parent? If much of our direction and instruction as a teacher sounds to be in Parent mode, is it any wonder we get a Child's response! Whilst the words might indeed be in Parent mode, the body language and tone needn't be. This is why non-verbal communication is so essential to being a teacher. Like dogs, we all tend to respond quickly to tone and body language.

Building a strong Adult (Harris, 1973)

- Learn to recognise your Child, its vulnerabilities, its fears, its principal methods of expressing these feelings.
- Learn to recognise your Parent, its admonitions, injunctions, fixed positions and principal ways of expressing these admonitions, injunctions, and positions.
- Be sensitive to the Child in others, talk to that Child, stroke that Child, protect that Child and appreciate its need for creative expression as well as the 'Not OK' burden it carries about.
- Count to ten, if necessary, in order to give the Adult time to process the incoming data, to sort out Parent and Child from reality.
- When in doubt, leave it out. You can't be attacked for what you didn't say.
- Work out a system of values. You can't make decisions without an ethical framework.'

Using Action Research

'Being a critically reflective practitioner is taking up a questioning disposition towards what teachers and schools actually do and want to do. It is questioning the ways individual and collective teacher actions are liberated and constrained by 'local' structures and the wider 'system' within which teachers work.'
Ghaye A. and K., 1998

This reflective approach may help you to mediate creatively your own induction year. When you are observed, whose agenda will it be, yours or your tutor's? You need feedback, both confirmatory to let you know you are on course and that things are going

well, and corrective feedback which should focus on and emphasise changing things so that you can improve your current practice. Ideally, you should encourage two types of feedback. 'First, to help you manage your work effectively, competently and ethically by offering new perspectives on things and by opening up unnoticed possibilities and alternatives. Secondly, feedback should help you become better at helping you to move your own thinking and practice forward.' (Adapted from Ghaye A. and K., 1998)

Action research is concerned with creating a good social order. The intended outcome is social justice through intervention for social reform, and the pedagogical aims are empowerment and critical citizenship.

The four moments of action research (Lewin, 1946)

Plan: Develop a plan of action to improve what is already happening.
Act: Act to implement the plan.
Observe: Observe the effects of the action in the context in which it occurs.
Reflect: Reflect on these as a catalyst for further planning and subsequent action.
Note that Action is followed by Research, which is followed by Action and further Research and so on; hence 'Action Research'.

Inherent in all this is Dewey's concept of viewing teaching or indeed any profession as 'problematic'. That is, we as teachers should question, look systematically and try to learn from our teaching and the children's learning as well as our own. Reflective Practice (See Schon, 1983) requires reflective turns. This means that we <u>re</u>-turn to <u>re</u>-view, <u>re</u>-see and <u>re</u>-search what it is that we do in our working lives, so that we can gain a more holistic view.

Listen for the Adult voice or actor and try to use it yourself. Recognise the Parent and Child being used by those you work with. "Yes, but!" "We have always done it this way!" "It's not fair!" "Get on and do as you are told."

I believe that we should not dwell on the problems that we and our children face, but try to understand them by peeling back the layers. By looking deeply at their nature, we can see them for what they really are. It is too easy to moan and groan, accept traditional views about low expectations and do nothing but worry and agonise over children's lack of progress. Instead, we can take some aspect of our work that puzzles us, appears problematic or feels as if it could be better. Then, by working on it to understand it, perhaps we can gain insights into the problem, let go of our cravings, habits, restlessness, distractions and see with clarity the reality of situation. Talk to your induction tutor about how you can use Action Research in your teaching to help you to become a reflective practitioner.

Chapter 10

YOUR SECOND YEAR

'Before I started my induction year, I was worried that I wouldn't be able to deal with all of the practical issues, including the pupils' parents, but I found that the school had good systems in place to deal with any problems, and my induction tutor helped me throughout the first year. I'm really looking forward to my second year.'

NQT at the start of the second year

Chapter contents:

■ **Setting targets for your second year**

■ **What are your INSET needs now?**

■ **What more can you offer the school?**

Setting targets for your second year

Well, you have survived your first year, and have hopefully benefited from quality feedback on your teaching and general involvement in the life of the school. Now is the time to take stock of what you have achieved, what direction you are moving in and reflect on your first year. You could use your Career Entry Profile again to develop a new action plan. We rarely manage to do everything on our wish list. Sometimes we find we need things we didn't even know existed. Are there still relevant needs which are unsatisfied on your CEP? How might these be satisfied? Discuss targets for your second year with your induction tutor and other colleagues, for example the headteacher, the INSET co-ordinator, or your department head.

What are your INSET needs now?

A good balanced way of establishing what these needs are might be to:

- **Find a good book, publication, video or web site** to work on over the summer.
- **Work with colleagues in school** on an aspect which you have identified as a personal professional need and which matches work the school is doing, such as developing curriculum materials, planning or building up a resource base, reviewing software or gathering resources from the Internet.
- **Attend local or school-based INSET.** Make sure it is what you really want, ask colleagues if they have been on similar courses by the provider.
- **Go to a conference,** probably organised by a professional body. Attending a conference could provide you with a source of inspiration for many years to come.

You might get involved in producing a poster, writing a paper or joining an action group. Look around and ask around. Ask colleagues what forms of in-service have proved to be most beneficial to them. You might even be able to contribute and take part, which should reduce or eliminate the cost. Do you want to engage in further study? Most new TTA funded courses demand an assignment if you get an assisted place. This could count towards an eventual Certificate, Diploma or Masters Degree. The steps are very gradual and well worth considering, sooner rather than later. You will meet like minded colleagues and hopefully be inspired and enthused.

What more can you offer the school?

Review your first year by asking yourself the following questions:

- Which activities and involvement have you welcomed and valued this year?
- How have they helped you to develop as a teacher?
- How have they influenced pupils' learning?
- Which relationships accord strongly with your beliefs and values as a teacher? Can you strengthen both the relationships and your beliefs and values? Have they changed?
- Is there more or less tension between what kind of teacher you would like to be and the teacher you actually see yourself to be? Who might help you?
- Can you see openings that would benefit both you and the school?

Remember my warning at the start. Don't take on too much. Look at the pattern of the year and try to work out if you can cope with greater involvement in certain areas at certain times. A guarded "Maybe; I'd like to. I'm really interested, but I don't know yet if I can fit it in." is often preferable to a gushing "Yes", which turns into a "Sorry, I just can't!" nearer the time.

Show initiative; ask yourself if you can imagine yourself involved in organising:

- sports day (only one day, a fixed date but it might rain);
- a lunchtime club one day per week (you might end up taking a chess team to matches twice a month or organising an ICT open evening for parents);
- netball training and coaching for the whole school (a major undertaking in terms of time and energy).

Think about the benefits and the sacrifices for both you and the school. You could do this using SWOT or PMI techniques (See Chapter 3). How can you develop those values that you care about? What more can you offer? Are there areas of involvement that you feel you have been misguided about in some way? Can you re-direct, reduce or avoid these?

Think about the following areas and who might help you to advance, retreat or stand firm in your involvement in:

- curriculum development. (Are you involved enough in subjects that you care about?);
- the School Development Plan. (How does this affect you? What about next year?);
- extra-curricular activities. (You need to aim for a balanced approach. Get a life!);
- pastoral care, the PTA, the Governing Body. (Are you ready for these?).

Aim for a balanced involvement across these three areas:

- planning, implementing and evaluating a curriculum area;
- an aspect of the life of the school;
- an extra-curricular activity.

Consider offering involvement in the form of a strength in some personally held value which evidences itself in action such as an interest in a particular charity, homelessness, substance abuse, first aid, environmental issues and so on. I have had a long involvement with OXFAM and the now thankfully redundant Anti-Apartheid Movement. I believe that teachers should try to help their pupils towards an informed world view. Children working out of school time to help those less fortunate than themselves, and knowing why they are doing it, has always been important for me. Learning that there are at least two sides to every case and that conciliation and forgiveness require perseverance and bravery is a valuable preparation for later life.

In order to sustain a career in teaching, I believe that you need to develop a coherent personal theory of education that is in line with your vision, values and ideals, and to commit yourself to lifelong learning. You have completed the first and major part of the transition from student to teacher. Try to remember what it felt like to be a pupil. Enjoy a well-earned rest and prepare yourself to do it all again, but this time with the wisdom and insights gained from your induction year as an NQT.

Appendix A – The Traffic Light System: Assessing your development

Use the traffic light system to show what is blocking you (**red**); what is temporarily holding you up (**amber**); and what you are already able to do (**green**). You cannot be assessed in areas in which you have no chance to show your ability. Work on those that you feel most comfortable with, then see what is left.

Standards	Red	Amber	Green
a. sets clear targets for improvement of pupils' achievement, monitors pupils' progress towards those targets and uses appropriate teaching strategies in the light of this, including, where appropriate, in relation to literacy, numeracy and other school targets;			
Sets clear targets for improvement of pupils' achievement			
Monitors pupils' progress towards those targets			
Uses teaching strategies to help realise individual and school targets			
b. plans effectively to ensure that pupils have the opportunity to meet their potential, notwithstanding differences of race and gender, and taking account of the needs of pupils who are underachieving, very able or not yet fluent in English;			
Plans to ensure that pupils have the opportunity to reach their potential			
Does not use stereotypes of race or gender to limit personal growth			
Takes account of the needs of pupils who are underachieving, very able or not yet fluent in English			
c. secures a good standard of pupil behaviour in the classroom through establishing appropriate rules and high expectations of discipline which pupils respect, acting to pre-empt and deal with inappropriate behaviour in the context of the behaviour policy of the school;			
Establishes appropriate rules			
Uses the behaviour policy of the school			
Secures a good standard of pupil behaviour in the classroom			
Has high expectations of discipline which pupils respect			
Acts to pre-empt and deal with inappropriate behaviour			
d. plans effectively, where applicable, to meet the needs of pupils with Special Educational Needs and, in collaboration with the SENCO, makes an appropriate contribution to the preparation, implementation, monitoring and review of Individual Education Plans;			
Plans effectively to meet the needs of pupils with Special Educational Needs			
Makes an appropriate contribution to the preparation, implementation, monitoring and review of Individual Education Plans, in collaboration with the SENCO			

Standards	Red	Amber	Green
e. takes account of ethnic and cultural diversity to enrich the curriculum and raise achievement;			
By celebrating ethnic and cultural diversity			
Enriches the curriculum and raises achievement			
f. recognises the level that a pupil is achieving and makes accurate assessments, independently, against attainment targets, where applicable, and performance levels associated with other tests or qualifications relevant to the subject(s) or phase(s) taught;			
Recognises the level that a pupil is achieving			
Makes independent accurate assessments against attainment targets			
Uses performance levels from other relevant tests or qualifications			
g. liaises effectively with pupils' parents/carers through informative oral and written reports on pupils' progress and achievements, discussing appropriate targets, and encouraging them to support their children's learning, behaviour and progress;			
Communicates effectively with pupils' parents/carers through informative oral and written reports on pupils' progress and achievements, discussing appropriate targets			
Encourages them to support their children's learning, behaviour and progress			
h. where applicable, deploys support staff and other adults effectively in the classroom, involving them, where appropriate, in the planning and management of pupils' learning;			
Deploys support staff and other adults effectively in the classroom			
Involves them in the planning and management of pupils' learning			
i. takes responsibility for implementing school policies and practices, including those dealing with bullying and racial harassment;			
Implements school policies and practices			
Especially those dealing with bullying and racial harassment			
j. takes responsibility for their own professional development, setting objectives for improvements, and taking action to keep up-to-date with research and developments in pedagogy and in the subject(s) they teach.			
Sets targets for improvements, and takes action to develop professionally			
Aware of recent research and developments in pedagogy and own subject			

Appendix B – Some resources to help you to reach the standards

You cannot be assessed in areas in which you have no chance to show your ability. Work on those you feel most comfortable with, then see what is left. Use this book, other texts and the Internet to support your progress and development. Share what you find with your induction tutor and other NQTs; swap resources.

Standards	This book	Other texts	Web sites
a. sets clear targets for improvement of pupils' achievement, monitors pupils' progress towards those targets and uses appropriate teaching strategies in the light of this, including, where appropriate, in relation to literacy, numeracy and other school targets;			
Sets clear targets for improvement of pupils' achievement	Chapters 2 and 5	Intros to NNS and NLS Pollard A. (1996) Smith A. (1996 / 1998) Joyce B. *et al.* (1997) Selley N. (1999)	www.dfee.gov.uk www.eduweb.co.uk www.topmarks.co.uk www.kidsdomain.co.uk
Monitors pupils' progress towards those targets	Chapter 5		
Uses teaching strategies to help realise individual and school targets	Chapters 6 and 8		
b. plans effectively to ensure that pupils have the opportunity to meet their potential, notwithstanding differences of race and gender, and taking account of the needs of pupils who are underachieving, very able or not yet fluent in English;			
Plans to ensure that pupils have the opportunity to reach their potential	Chapters 2, 4, 5 and 6	Pollard A. (1997) Blagg N. (1988) Claxton (1999) Holt J. (1984) Estes C.P. (1993) Teare B. (1999) Williams D. (1992, etc)	www.elib.com/Steiner www.taruna.gen.nz/anthroposophy.html www.tut-world.com/ www.nasen.org.uk/links/home.htm/
Does not use stereotypes of race or gender to limit personal growth	Chapters 2, 7 and 8		
Takes account of the needs of pupils who are underachieving, very able or not yet fluent in English	Chapters 2, 6, 7, 8 and 9		
c. secures a good standard of pupil behaviour in the classroom through establishing appropriate rules and high expectations of discipline which pupils respect, acting to pre-empt and deal with inappropriate behaviour in the context of the behaviour policy of the school;			
Establishes appropriate rules	Chapters 4 and 7	Bennet N. (1992) Laslett R. (1992) MacManus M. (1990) Merret F. (1990) Munn P. (1992) Moseley J. (1995) Relf P. *et al.* (1998) Watkins C. (2000)	www.mentors.net www.teachermentors.net www.isma.org.uk/mindmaps www.askatl.org.uk/issues www.luckyduck.co.uk www.teachers.org.uk www.antidote.org.uk
Uses the behaviour policy of the school	Chapter 4		
Secures a good standard of pupil behaviour in the classroom	Chapters 2, 4 and 9		
Has high expectations of discipline which pupils respect	Chapters 2 and 4		
Acts to pre-empt and deal with inappropriate behaviour	Chapters 2, 4 and 9		
d. plans effectively, where applicable, to meet the needs of pupils with Special Educational Needs and, in collaboration with the SENCO, makes an appropriate contribution to the preparation, implementation, monitoring and review of Individual Education Plans;			
Plans effectively to meet the needs of pupils with Special Educational Needs	Chapters 3, 4, 5 and 8	Bloomfield A. (1997) Capel S. *et al.* (1997) Dickinson C. (1996) Sharron H. (1994) Vitale (1992) Williams D. (1997)	www.highscope.org/abomain.html www.bobnancy.com/welcome.html www.nasen.org.uk
Makes an appropriate contribution to the preparation, implementation, monitoring and review of Individual Education Plans, in collaboration with the SENCO	Chapters 2, 5, 6 and 7		

Standards	This book	Other texts	Web sites
e. takes account of ethnic and cultural diversity to enrich the curriculum and raise achievement;			
By celebrating ethnic and cultural diversity	Chapter 2	Phinn G. (1998) Pike G. and Selby D. (1988) Weigand P. (1992)	www.ibo.org.uk www.actden.com/index.html www.bernardvanleer.org www.wwfleaning.co.uk
Enriches the curriculum and raises achievement	Chapters 5, 6 and 8		
f. recognises the level that a pupil is achieving and makes accurate assessments, independently, against attainment targets, where applicable, and performance levels associated with other tests or qualifications relevant to the subject(s) or phase(s) taught;			
Recognises the level that a pupil is achieving	Chapters 5 and 6	Hughes M.(1999) Tripp D. (1993) White R. and Gunstone R. (1992) Headington R. (2000)	www.standards.dfee.gov.uk www.sofweb.vic.edu.au/assess /kla.htmss/kla.htm www.qlsi.com www.studyweb.com
Makes independent accurate assessments against attainment targets	Chapters 2 and 5		
Uses performance levels from other relevant tests or qualifications	Chapters 1 and 5		
g. liaises effectively with pupils' parents/carers through informative oral and written reports on pupils' progress and achievements, discussing appropriate targets, and encouraging them to support their children's learning, behaviour and progress;			
Communicates effectively with pupils' parents/carers through informative oral and written reports on pupils' progress and achievements, discussing appropriate targets	Chapters 2, 3, 5 and 9	Goleman D. (1996) Harris T.A. (1973) Holt J. (1984, 1986)	www.merseyworld.com/sthelens-parents/ www.parenting.org.uk/index.html www.educate.co.uk www.schoolzone.co.uk
Encourages them to support their children's learning, behaviour and progress	Chapters 2, 5, 6 and 9		
h. where applicable, deploys support staff and other adults effectively in the classroom, involving them, where appropriate, in the planning and management of pupils' learning;			
Deploys support staff and other adults effectively in the classroom	Chapters 1, 3 and 6	Moyles J. (1992) Mc Grath M. (2000) Field K. et al. (2000)	www.teach-tta.gov.uk www.cleo.ucsm.ac.uk www.4learning.co.uk
Involves them in the planning and management of pupils' learning	Chapters 2, 3, 4 and 5		
i. takes responsibility for implementing school policies and practices, including those dealing with bullying and racial harassment;			
Implements school policies and practices	Chapters 1 and 4	MacGilchrist et al. (1997)	www.childline.org.uk www.bullying.co.uk www.teachernet.gov.uk
Especially those dealing with bullying and racial harassment	Chapter 4	DfE (1994)	
j. takes responsibility for their own professional development, setting objectives for improvements, and taking action to keep up-to-date with research and developments in pedagogy and in the subject(s) they teach.			
Sets targets for improvements, and takes action to develop professionally	Chapters 3, 5, 6 and 9	Askew M. (1995) Ghaye A. and K. (1998) Pollard A. (1996)	www.edwdebono.com/ www.triangle.co.uk/ciec
Aware of recent research and developments in pedagogy and own subject	Chapters 9 and 10		

Appendix C – Bibliography

Author	Year	Title	Publisher	Chapter links
Acres D.	1994	How to Pass Exams Without Anxiety (3rd edition)	How To Books	3
Amos J.	1998	Managing Your Time	How To Books	3
Anderson R.	1999	First Steps to a Physical Basis of Concentration	Crown House Publishing	4, 5
Askew M.	1995	Recent Research in Maths Education 5 - 16	HMSO	8
Atkinson S. (Ed.)	1992	Mathematics with Reason: The Emergent Approach to Primary Mathematics	Hodder and Stoughton	8
ATM	1985	Notes on Mathematics for Children	ATM (CUP)	1
ATM	1987	'Away with Maths' Pack	ATM	2
Ben-Hur M.	1994	On Feuerstein's Instrumental Enrichment	IRI Skylight	4, 8
Bennett N. and Dunne E.	1992	Managing Classroom Groups	Simon and Schuster	3, 4
Berne E.	1961	Transactional Analysis in Psychotherapy	Grove Press	9
Berne E.	1964	Games People Play	Grove Press	9
Blagg N. et al.	1988	Somerset Thinking Skills Course	Blackwell	8
Bloomfield A.	1997	People Maths	S. Thornes Ltd	3
Bruner J.	1966	Towards a Theory of Instruction	Harvard	7
Buzan T.	1991	Use Your Perfect Memory	Penguin	8
Buzan T.	1993	Mind Map Book	BBC Books	8
Buzan T.	1995	Use Your Head	BBC Books	8
Capel S. et al.	1997	Starting to Teach in the Secondary School	Routledge	General
Carr W. and Kemmis S.	1986	Becoming Critical: Education, Knowledge and Action Research	Routledge	9
Carter R.	1998	Mapping the Mind	Weidenfeld and Nicolson	General
Claxton G.	1990	Teaching to Learn: a Direction for Education	Cassell	8
Claxton G.	1998	Hare Brain Tortoise Mind	Fourth Estate	General
Claxton G.	1999	Wise up: The Challenge of Lifelong Learning	Bloomsbury	6, 7, 8
De Bono E.	1971	The Dog-Exercising Machine	Penguin	8
De Bono E.	1992	Teach Your Child How to Think	Viking	
De Bono E.	1994	Parallel Thinking	Viking	6
De Bono E.	1998	Simplicity	Viking (Penguin)	3
Dennison P. and G.	1986	Brain Gym	Edu-kinaesthetics	2
DES	1989	Discipline in Schools (Elton Report)	HMSO	4

Author	Year	Title	Publisher	Chapter links
Dewey J.	1933	How We Think: A Restatement of the Relation of Reflective Thinking to the Educative Process	Henry Regnery	General
DfE	1994	Bullying: Don't Suffer in Silence	HMSO	4
Dickinson C.	1996	Effective Learning Activities	Network Educational Press	2, 6
Druikurs R.	1957	Psychology in the Classroom	Staples Press	General
Estes	1993	Women who Run with Wolves	Rider	General
Feuerstein R.	1983	Instrumental Enrichment	University Park Press	6, 7, 8
Field K et al.	2000	Effective Subject Leadership	Routledge	5, 6 ,8, 9
Fisher R.	1990	Teaching children to think	Blackwell	8
Fisher R.	1995	Teaching children to learn	S Thornes	3
Fontana D.	1986	Classroom Control	Methuen	4
Gardner H.	1983	Frames of Mind: The theory of multiple intelligences	Basic Books	8
Ghaye A. and Ghaye K.	1998	Teaching and Learning through Critical Reflective Practice	David Fulton Publishers	9
Gibran K.	1923	The Prophet	Heinemann	2
Glasser W.	1986	Choice Theory in the Classroom	Harper Perennial	4, 5, 8, 9
Goleman D.	1996	Emotional Intelligence	Bloomsbury	General
Greenfield S.	2000	The Private Life of the Brain	Allen Lane	7
Harris T.A.	1973	I'm OK, you're OK	Pan	9
Headington R.	2000	Monitoring, Assessment, Recording and Accountability	David Fulton	5
Holt J.	1984	How Children Fail	Pelican	General
Holt J.	1986	How Children Learn	Penguin	General
Honey P. and Mumford A.	1992	The Manual of Learning Styles	P. Honey	6
Hughes M.	1986	Children and Number	Blackwell	8
Hughes M.	1999	Closing The Learning Gap	Network Educational Press	General
James F. and Brownsword K.	1992	A Positive Approach, Creating a Learning Environment	Blair	General
Joyce B. et al.	1997	Models of Learning – Tools for Teaching	Open University Press	6
Kelmer-Pringle M.	1974	The Needs of Children	Hutchinson	4
Laslett R. and Smith C.	1992	Effective Classroom Mangement: A Teacher's Guide	Routledge	4
Lewin K.	1946	Action Research and Minority Problems	Journal of Social Issues, 2	9
Lewis A.	1996	Discovering Mathematics with 4 - 7 year olds	Hodder	8
Lipman M. et al.	1980	Philosophy in the classroom	Temple University Press	2
McCarthy B.	1983	The 4MAT System	EXCEL	8

Author	Year	Title	Publisher	Chapter links
MacGrath M.	2000	The Art of Peaceful Teaching	David Fulton	4, 5, 6, 8
McNiff J	1988	Action Research: Principles	Routledge	9
McNiff J	1992	Teachers as Learners	Routledge	General
MacGilchrist B. et al.	1997	The Intelligent School	Paul Chapman	General
MacLean P.	1978	'A mind of three minds, educating the triune brain', in Education and the Brain	Chicago University Press	7
MacManus M.	1989	Troublesome Behaviour in the Classroom	Routledge	4
Maines B.	1991	Challenging Behaviour in the Primary School	University of West of England	4
Maslow A.H.	1970	Motivation and Personality	Harper	4
Merret F. and Wheldall K.	1990	Positive Teaching in the Primary School	Paul Chapman	4
Merttens R.	1998	Simmering Activities	Ginn and Co	2
Moseley J.	1995	Circle Time	Lame Duck Publishing	2
Moyles J.	1992	Organising for Learning in the Primary Classroom	Open University Press	2, 3, 4
Munn P. et al.	1992	Effective Discipline in Primary Schools	Paul Chapman	4
Novak J. and Gowin V.	1984	Learning How to Learn	CUP	8
OFSTED	1992	The New Teacher in School	HMSO	General
Penfield W.	1977	No Man Alone: A Neurosurgeon's Life		9
Phinn G.	1998	The Other Side of the Dale	Penguin	Essential
Pike G. and Selby D.	1988	Global Teacher, Global Learner	Hodder and Stoughton	2
Pollard A.	1997	Reflective Teaching in the Primary School	Cassell	1, 9
Pollard A. (ed)	1996	Readings for Reflective Teaching	Cassell	General
Pound L.	1999	Supporting Mathematical Development in the Early Years	Open University Press	6
Purkey W.W.	1970	Self-Concept and School Achievement	Prentice Hall	4
Relf P., Hirst R., Richardson J. and Youdell G.	1998	Best Behaviour – Starting Points for effective behaviour management	Network Educational Press	4
Robbins A.	1988	Unlimited Power	Simon and Schuster	3
Schon D.A.	1983	The Reflective Practitioner: How Professionals Think in Action	Maurice Temple Smith	9
Selley N.	1999	The Art of Constructivist Teaching	David Fulton	6, 8, 9
Sharron H.	1994	Changing Children's Minds	Sharron	General
Smith A.	1996	Accelerated Learning in the Classroom	Network Educational Press	2, 7
Smith A.	1998	Accelerated Learning In Practice	Network Educational Press	4, 7
Sylwester R.	1995	A Celebration of Neurons	ASCD	7
Teare B.	1999	Effective Resources for Able and Talented Children	Network Educational Press	6

Author	Year	Title	Publisher	Chapter links
Tripp D.	1993	Critical Incidents in Teaching	Routledge	3
Vygotsky L.S.	1962	Thought and Language	MIT Press	7
Watkins C. and Wagner P.	2000	Improving School Behaviour	Paul Chapman	4
Weigand P.	1992	Places in the Primary School	Falmer	General
White R. and Gunstone R.	1992	Probing Understanding	Falmer	General
Williams D.	1992	Nobody Nowhere	Corgi	General
Williams D.	1994	Somebody Somewhere	Corgi	General
Williams D.	1997	Autism – An Inside Out Approach	Jessica Kingsley	General
Williams D.	1998	Autism and Sensing: the unlost instinct	Jessica Kingsley	5, 9
Wragg E.C.	1993	Class Management	Routledge	4

Appendix D – Web Sites

Web site	Description	(Ref to Standards)
Special Educational Needs	**Look for links from NGfL**	**(d)**
www.nas.org.uk	National Autistic Society	
www.rnib.org.uk/	Royal National Institute for the Blind	
www.rnid.org.uk/	Royal National Institute for the Deaf	
www.official-documents.co.uk/ document/ofsted/veryable/able-02a.htm	OFSTED Reviews of Research – Educating the very able	
www.nasen.org.uk/links/home.htm	Special educational needs links and information	
Equality and Justice	**Try Standards site.**	**(b, i, e)**
www.cedc.org.uk/	Community Education Development Centre. Widening participation.	
www.childline.org.uk/	Help and advice on bullying, racism, abuse….	
www.cie.org/	Council on Islamic Education. USA based. Resources and info.	
www.comicrelief.org.uk/	Look for the education section	
www.globalgang.org.uk/	Christian Aid's site for 7 – 12 yr olds. Global citizenship.	
www.multifaithnet.org/	Good place to start RE and cultural understanding	
www.indiatimes.com	Look under spirituality for world religions, festivals, answers….	
www.ort.org/	Fascinating philanthropic organisation founded by Russian Jews in 1880.	
www.drugscope.org.uk/	"Informing Policy, Reducing Risk." Extensive library….	
http://www.derby.ac.uk/telmie2/	Telematic European learning materials for inclusive education	
www.educationextra.org.uk	Out of school learning charity including Diana Awards info.	
Sustaining the Environment		**(c)**
www.greenchannel.com/areas.htm (Hosts numerous organisations)	Dedicated to positive environmental change by improved communication of information, products, services and initiatives..	
www.wwflearning.co.uk/ welcome/index.shtml	New WWF site, lifelong learning for a sustainable future.	
http://www.think-energy.com/links.html	Diverse energy saving sites	

Key Government Sites and Portals	NGfL is the real starting point	(j ...)
www.canteach.gov.uk/home.htm	TTA's comprehensive site for teachers	
www.teachernet.gov.uk	Major government portal. National Grid for Learning. START HERE	
www.ngfl.gov.uk/ngfl/index.html		
www.becta.org.uk/index.cfm	British Educational Communications & Technology agency	
www.coi.gov.uk	Central Office of Information	
www.dfee.gov.uk	Department for Education and Employment	
www.standards.dfee.gov.uk/	Major on-line teacher services. E.g. literacy, numeracy, gender, parents, EAZ	
www.vtc.ngfl.gov.uk	Virtual Teacher's Centre many links.	
www.wiredforhealth.gov.uk/	Starting point for health education issues. Links to 250 selected sites.	
www.staffordshire.gov.uk	LEA site. Lists NQTs. Try a different county name.	
www.cleo.ucsm.ac.uk/	Cumbria, Lancashire, education online. Visit and enjoy.	
www.primaryresources.co.uk/	Edelston Primary School; good design, resources and links	

Media and other Resource Providers		(j ....)
www.4learning.co.uk/	Channel 4's impressive site. Try blackhistorymap, homeworkhigh	
www.bbc.co.uk/education/home/	Why re-invent the wheel when someone else has done it for you.	
www.bbc.co.uk/webguide	One of the best places to start searching for things on the web.	
www.bbc.co.uk/webwise/	Web virgins start here.	
stress.channel4.com/	A whole site devoted to helping you deal with stress. Interactive.	
www.topmarks.co.uk/	FREE respected site with excellent links and searching facilities. START	
www.teachers.ash.org.au/ teachereduc/default.html	Aussie Schoolhouse, links, resources and pedagogy	
www.eduweb.co.uk	Education Website Directory	
www.swopnet.com/ed/index.html	Starter activities. Lots of resources	
www.tut-world.com/	Worksheets and tutorials galore	
www.think.com/	A powerful free site run by Oracle. You must register. Many parts.	
www.actden.com/index.htm	Digital Education Network, free tutorials	
www.digitalbrain.com/	Some free online training plus a host of facilities. Must see!	
www.angliacampus.com/	Major provider of online service to education	
www.education-net.co.uk/	Education Marketplace conferences e.g. BETT, info, articles, links	

www.studyweb.com/	US study web selection; high standards
www.qlsi.com	Quality Learning Systems International
www.theschoolbook.co.uk/	Very new Swedish online resource purchasing portal?
webpages.marshall.edu/ ~jmullens/edlinks.html	A serious USA site for educational links
www.j-sainsbury.co.uk/museum	Virtual museum; history portal

Parents & Children	Look in Standards site	(g)
www.merseyworld.com/ sthelens-parents/	Partnership with parents in Newton	
www.parenting.org.uk/index.html	Positive parenting	
www.schoolzone.co.uk	Information & resources for teachers, parents and children	
www.educate.co.uk	Information & support for parents, teachers and children	
www.soton.ac.uk/~jrc3/chudler/ neurok.html	Neuroscience for kids	
www.kidsdomain.co.uk/index.html	Lots to do for kids. Adults and parents sections also.	

Models of Teaching, Learning and Curriculum	Look in NGfL, QLSI,	(a, b, e, j)
www.i4.auc.dk/rask/itbibs/education.htm	Danish education site	
www.ibo.org.uk/ibo/english/index.cfm	International Baccalaureat Organisation	
icdl.open.ac.uk/	International Centre for Distance Learning	
www.open.ac.uk/frames.html	The Open University	
www.buzancentre.com/TBuzan.html	Tony Buzan's Business Centre	
www.braindance.com/homepage.htm	The home of Tony Buzan's "Braindance"	
www.edwdebono.com/	Edward De Bono home pages. Thinking Skills, Lateral Thinking , Neuroscience	
www.qlsi.com/educate_direct/ie/	Instrumental Enrichment overview from Quality Learning Systems Inc.	
www.thehopecharity.org.uk/reuven.htm	Professor Reuven Feuerstein	
www.ed.psu.edu/insys/ESD/ Gardner/menu.html	Gardner	
www.edge.org/3rd_culture/ bios/gardner.html	Gardner	
www.highscope.org/abomain.htm	Highscope	
www.newhorizons.org	Neuroscience and Education. Must see!	
www.poky.srv.net/~angels/index.html/ presuppositions.html	NLP presuppositions	
www.ozemail.com.au/~cromhale/links.html	Australian Steiner Education plus links	
members.aol.com/ERSschool/index.htm	Edinburgh Rudolf Steiner School	

www.taruna.gen.nz/anthroposophy.html	Steiner in New Zealand	
www.elib.com/Steiner/	Rudolph Steiner Archives	
www.bobnancy.com/welcome.html	Rudolph Steiner stuff	
www.sapere.net	Home of Philosophy for children	
www.antidote.org.uk	Emotional Literacy & lots more	

Specific Curriculum Sites (exemplars)	**Look in NGfL**	**(j)**
www1.oup.co.uk/equipe/	Learn French on the web.	
www.mesopotamia.co.uk/	Example of a British Museum self-contained site.	
www.thebritishmuseum.ac.uk/	A huge resource. Spend a day browsing.	
www.colormathpink.com/	Great US maths site to encourage girls and women into maths. Many US maths links.	
www.mathsyear2000.org/	Good free maths site. Likely to be updated.	
www.schoolscience.co.uk/content/index.asp	Leading free site for science.	

Assessment	**Look in NGfL, OFSTED, Unions**	**(a, d. f)**
www.sofweb.vic.edu.au/assess/kla.htm	Assessment and reporting Australian style.	
www.ozemail.com/~caveman/Creative/Mindmap/index.html	Mindmaps	
www.isma.org.uk/mindmaps.htm	Stress management with mindmaps	
www.fairness.freeserve.co.uk/ta.html	Transactional Analysis	

Early Years		
www.triangle.co.uk/ciec	Contemporary issues in early childhood – online journal	
www.bernardvanleer.org	Early childhood matters	
www.mentors.net	Association for Supervision and Curriculum Development (ASCD)	

Recruitment and Jobs	**Keep looking, frequent changes**	**(j)**
www.eteach.com/	Recruitment, news, articles	
www.education-jobs.co.uk/	Recruitment and jobs	
www.teachingworld.co.uk/		
www.jobs.tes.co.uk/		
www.aft.co.uk/		
www.jobsunlimited.co.uk/		
www.centralbureau.org.uk	Central Bureau for International Education and Training	

Managing Behaviour & Unions	A bit of digging will help.	(c, i, j)
www.askatl.org.uk/issues/managing_classroom_behaviour.htm	A complete booklet on the web. Ask ATL	
www.nfer.ac.uk/subject/behaviour.htm	Extensive book list. Many other topics.	
www.luckyduck.co.uk/behaviourmlist.html	Another friendlier list of classroom advice.	
www.gtce.org.uk/	General Teaching Council site.	
www.teachersunion.org.uk/	NASWT's organised goodies	
www.teachers.org.uk/	NUT's growing site. Advice for NQTs	
www.askatl.org.uk/issues/bullying_at_work.htm	ATL's ask site on bullying at work.	
www.stress.org.uk/bullying.htm	Workplace Bullying report. Stress management site.	
www.bullying.co.uk/	Web-site dedicated to bullying. Those who can do. Those who can't bully.	
www.bbc.co.uk/education/archive/bully/	Comprehensive guide on bullying.	
www.successunlimited.co.uk/links.htm	Huge list of links on Bullying world-wide	

Teacherline   0800 562561

Phone up about ANY problem you are having 24 hours a day, 7 days a week.

INDEX

Other Titles from Network Educational Press

THE SCHOOL EFFECTIVENESS SERIES

Getting Started *is book 14 of The School Effectiveness Series, which focuses on practical and useful ideas for individual schools and teachers. The series addresses the issues of whole school improvement along with new knowledge about teaching and learning, and offers straightforward solutions that teachers can use to make life more rewarding for themselves and those they teach.*

Book 1: *Accelerated Learning in the Classroom* by Alistair Smith
- The first book in the UK to apply new knowledge about the brain to classroom practice
- Contains practical methods so teachers can apply accelerated learning theories to their own classrooms
- Aims to increase the pace of learning and deepen understanding
- Includes advice on how to create the ideal environment for learning and how to help learners fulfil their potential
- Full of lively illustrations, diagrams and plans
- Offers practical solutions on improving performance, motivation and understanding
- Contains a checklist of action points for the classroom – 21 ways to improve learning

Book 2: *Effective Learning Activities* by Chris Dickinson
- An essential teaching guide which focuses on practical activities to improve learning
- Aims to improve results through effective learning, which will raise achievement, deepen understanding, promote self-esteem and improve motivation
- Includes activities which are designed to promote differentiation and understanding
- Offers advice on how to maximise the use of available – and limited – resources
- Includes activities suitable for GCSE, National Curriculum, Highers, GSVQ and GNVQ
- From the author of the highly acclaimed 'Differentiation: A Practical Handbook of Classroom Strategies'

Book 3: *Effective Heads of Department* by Phil Jones & Nick Sparks
- An ideal support for Heads of Department looking to develop necessary management skills
- Contains a range of practical systems and approaches; each of the eight sections ends with a 'checklist for action'
- Designed to develop practice in line with OFSTED expectations and DfEE thinking by monitoring and improving quality
- Addresses issues such as managing resources, leadership, learning, departmental planning and making assessment valuable
- Includes useful information for Senior Managers in schools who are looking to enhance the effectiveness of their Heads of Department

Book 4: *Lessons are for Learning* by Mike Hughes
- Brings together the theory of learning with the realities of the classroom environment
- Encourages teachers to reflect on their own classroom practice and challenges them to think about why they teach in the way they do
- Develops a clear picture of what constitutes effective classroom practice
- Offers practical suggestions for activities that bridge the gap between recent developments in the theory of learning and the constraints of classroom teaching
- Ideal for stimulating thought and generating discussion
- Written by a practising teacher who has also worked as a teaching advisor, a PGCE co-ordinator and an OFSTED inspector

Book 5: *Effective Learning in Science* by Paul Denley and Keith Bishop
- Looks at planning for effective learning within the context of science
- Encourages discussion about the aims and purposes in teaching science and the role of subject knowledge in effective teaching
- Tackles issues such as planning for effective learning, the use of resources and other relevant management issues
- Offers help in the development of a departmental plan to revise schemes of work, resources and classroom strategies, in order to make learning and teaching more effective
- Ideal for any science department aiming to increase performance and improve results

Book 6: *Raising Boys' Achievement* by Jon Pickering
- Addresses the causes of boys' underachievement and offers possible solutions
- Focuses the search for causes and solutions on teachers working in the classrooms
- Looks at examples of good practice in schools to help guide the planning and implementation of strategies to raise achievement
- Offers practical, 'real' solutions along with tried and tested training suggestions
- Ideal as a basis for INSET or as a guide to practical activities for classroom teachers

Book 7: *Effective Provision for Able & Talented Children* by Barry Teare
- Basic theory, necessary procedures and turning theory into practice
- Main methods of identifying the able and talented
- Concerns about achievement and appropriate strategies to raise achievement
- The role of the classroom teacher, monitoring and evaluation techniques
- Practical enrichment activities and appropriate resources

Book 8: *Effective Careers Education & Guidance* by Andrew Edwards and Anthony Barnes
- Strategic planning of the careers programme as part of the wider curriculum
- Practical consideration of managing careers education and guidance
- Practical activities for reflection and personal learning, and case studies where such activities have been used
- Aspects of guidance and counselling involved in helping students to understand their own capabilities and form career plans
- Strategies for reviewing and developing existing practice

Book 9: *Best behaviour and Best behaviour FIRST AID* by
Peter Relf, Rod Hirst, Jan Richardson and Georgina Youdell
- Provides support for those who seek starting points for effective behaviour management, for individual teachers and for middle and senior managers
- Focuses on practical and useful ideas for individual schools and teachers

Best behaviour FIRST AID
(pack of 5 booklets)
- Provides strategies to cope with aggression, defiance and disturbance
- Straightforward action points for self-esteem

Book 10: *The Effective School Governor* by David Marriott
(including free audio tape)
- Straightforward guidance on how to fulfil a governor's role and responsibilities
- Develops your personal effectiveness as an individual governor
- Practical support on how to be an effective member of the governing team
- Audio tape for use in car or at home

Book 11: *Improving Personal Effectiveness for Managers in Schools* by James Johnson
- An invaluable resource for new and experienced teachers in both primary and secondary schools
- Contains practical strategies for improving leadership and management skills
- Focuses on self-management skills, managing difficult situations, working under pressure, developing confidence, creating a team ethos and communicating effectively

Book 12: *Making Pupil Data Powerful* by Maggie Pringle and Tony Cobb

- Shows teachers in primary, middle and secondary schools how to interpret pupils' performance data and how to use it to enhance teaching and learning
- Provides practical advice on analysing performance and learning behaviours, measuring progress, predicting future attainment, setting targets and ensuring continuity and progression
- Explains how to interpret national initiatives on data-analysis, benchmarking and target-setting, and to ensure that these have value in the classroom

Book 13: *Closing the Learning Gap* by Mike Hughes

- Helps teachers, departments and schools to close the Learning Gap between what we know about effective learning and what actually goes on in the classroom
- Encourages teachers to reflect on the ways in which they teach, and to identify and implement strategies for improving their practice
- Helps teachers to apply recent research findings about the brain and learning
- Full of practical advice and real, tested strategies for improvement
- Written by a teacher, for teachers, to stimulate thought and interest 'at a glance'

Book 15: *Leading the Learning School* by Colin Weatherley

The main theme is that the effective leadership of true 'learning schools' involves applying the principles of learning to all levels of educational management:

- Learning – 13 key principles of learning are derived from a survey of up-to-date knowledge of the brain and learning
- Teaching – how to use the key principles of learning to improve teachers' professional knowledge and skills, make the learning environment more supportive and improve the design of learning activities
- Staff Development – how the same principles that should underpin the design and teaching of learning activities for pupils should underpin the design and provision of development activities for teachers
- Organizational Development – how a learning school should be consciously managed according to these same key principles of learning. The section proposes a radical new 'whole brain' approach to Development Planning

Book 16: *Adventures in Learning* by Mike Tilling

- Integrate other theories about how we learn into a coherent 'vision' of learning that unfolds over time
- Recognise the phases of the Learner's Journey and make practical interventions at key moments
- Shape the experience of learners from the 'micro' level of the individual lesson to the 'macro' level of the learning lifetime

Book 17: *Strategies for Closing the Learning Gap* by Mike Hughes with Andy Vass

- Highlights and simplifies key issues emerging from the latest discoveries about how the human brain learns
- Offers proven, practical strategies and suggestions as to how to apply this new research in the classroom, to improve students' learning and help them achieve their full potential
- Written and arranged in the same easy-to-read style as *Closing the Learning Gap*, to encourage teachers to browse through it during 'spare' moments

Book 18: *Classroom Management* by Philip Waterhouse and Chris Dickinson

- Classic best-selling text by Philip Waterhouse, set in the current context by Chris Dickinson
- Full of practical ideas to help teachers find ways of integrating Key Skills and Thinking Skills into an already overcrowded curriculum
- Shows how Induction Standards, OFSTED requirements and the findings of the Hay McBer report into School Effectiveness can be met or implemented through carefully thought out strategies for the management and organisation of the classroom
- Covers topics including whole-class presentation, dialogue and interactive teaching; teacher-led small group work; classroom layout; interpersonal relationships in the classroom; and collaborative teamwork

ACCELERATED LEARNING SERIES

General Editor: **Alistair Smith**

Accelerated Learning in Practice by Alistair Smith

- The author's second book, which takes Nobel Prize winning brain research into the classroom.
- Structured to help readers access and retain the information necessary to begin to accelerate their own learning and that of the students they teach.
- Contains over 100 learning tools, case studies from 36 schools and an up-to-the-minute resource section
- Includes nine principles of learning based on brain research and the author's seven-stage Accelerated Learning Cycle.

The ALPS Approach: Accelerated Learning in Primary Schools

by Alistair Smith and Nicola Call

- Shows how research on how we learn, collected by Alistair Smith, can be used to great effect in the primary classroom.
- Provides practical and accessible examples of strategies used by highly experienced primary teacher Nicola Call, at a school where the SATs results shot up as a consequence.
- Professional, practical and exhilarating resource that gives readers the opportunity to develop the ALPS approach for themselves and for the children in their care.
- The ALPS approach includes: Exceeding expectation, 'Can-do' learning, Positive performance, Target-setting that works, Using review for recall, Preparing for tests … and much more.

MapWise by Oliver Caviglioli and Ian Harris

- Provides informed access to the most powerful accelerated learning technique around – Model Mapping.
- Shows how mapping can be used to address National Curriculum thinking skills requirements for students of any preferred learning style by infusing thinking into subject teaching.
- Describes how mapping can be used to measure and develop intelligence.
- Explains how mapping supports teacher explanation and student understanding.
- Demonstrates how mapping makes planning, teaching and reviewing easier and more effective.
- Written and illustrated to be lively and engaging, practical and supportive.

The ALPS Resource Book by Alistair Smith and Nicola Call

- Follow-up to the authors' best-selling book *The ALPS Approach*, structured carefully to extend the theoretical and practical advice given in that publication.
- Provides a wealth of photocopiable, 'hands-on' resources for teachers to use in, and outside, the classroom.
- Describes over 1000 useful ideas for teachers to 'accelerate' children's learning, including affirmation posters for your classroom; how to make target-setting easy, fun and useful; rules and guidelines for positive behaviour; writing frames and thinking skills templates; how to help children better understand their brain and get it to work; advice on managing attention and dealing with groups; ten ways to improve test performance; sample school policies; 101 'brain break' activities that connect to learning.

EDUCATION PERSONNEL MANAGEMENT SERIES

These new Education Personnel Management handbooks will help headteachers, senior managers and governors to manage a broad range of personnel issues.

The Well Teacher – management strategies for beating stress, promoting staff health and reducing absence

by Maureen Cooper

- Provides straightforward, practical advice on how to deal strategically with staff absenteeism, which can be so expensive in terms of sick pay and supply cover, through proactively promoting staff health.
- Includes suggestions for reducing stress levels in schools.
- Outlines ways in which to deal with individual cases of staff absence.

Managing Challenging People – dealing with staff conduct
by Bev Curtis and Maureen Cooper
- Deals with managing staff whose conduct gives cause for concern.
- Summarises the employment relationship in schools, as well as those areas of education and employment law relevant to staff discipline.
- Looks at the differences between conduct and capability, and between misconduct and gross misconduct.
- Describes disciplinary and dismissal procedures relating to teaching and non-teaching staff, including headteachers.
- Describes case studies and model procedures, and provides pro-forma letters to help schools with these difficult issues.

Managing Poor Performance – handling staff capability issues
by Bev Curtis and Maureen Cooper
- Explains clearly why capability is important in providing an effective and high quality education for pupils.
- Gives advice on how to identify staff with poor performance, and how to help them improve.
- Outlines the legal position and the role of governors in dealing with the difficult issues surrounding poor performance.
- Details the various stages of formal capability procedures and dismissal hearings.
- Describes case studies and model procedures, and provides pro-forma letters.

Managing Allegations Against Staff – personnel and child protection issues in schools
by Maureen Cooper
- Provides invaluable advice to headteachers, senior managers and personnel staff on how to deal with the difficult issues arising from accusations made against school employees.
- Shows what schools can do to protect students, while safeguarding employees from the potentially devastating consequences of false allegations.
- Describes real-life case studies.
- Provides a clear outline of the legal background plus a moral code of conduct for staff.

Managing Recruitment and Selection – appointing the best staff
by Bev Curtis and Maureen Cooper
- Guides schools through the legal minefield of anti-discrimination, human rights and other legislation relevant when making appointments.
- Provides senior managers and staffing committees with help in many areas, including developing effective selection procedures, creating job descriptions and personnel specifications, writing better job advertisements and short-listing and interviewing techniques.

Managing Redundancies – dealing with reduction and reorganisation of staff
by Bev Curtis and Maureen Cooper
- Provides guidance in how to handle fairly and carefully the unsettling and sensitive issue of making staff redundant.
- Gives independent advice on keeping staff informed of their options, employment and other relevant legislation, sources of support (including the LEA) and working to the required time-scales.

VISIONS OF EDUCATION SERIES

The Unfinished Revolution by John Abbott and Terry Ryan
- Draws on evidence from the past to show how shifting attitudes in society and politics have shaped Western education systems.
- Argues that what is now needed is a completely fresh approach, designed around evidence about how children actually learn.
- Describes a vision of an education system based on current research into how our brains work, and designed to encourage the autonomous and inventive thinkers and learners that the 21st century demands.
- Essential reading for anyone involved in education and policy making.

THE LITERACY COLLECTION

Helping With Reading by Anne Butterworth and Angela White
- Includes sections on 'Hearing Children Read', Word Recognition' and 'Phonics'.
- Provides precisely focused, easily implemented follow-up activities for pupils who need extra reinforcement of basic reading skills.
- Provides clear, practical and easily implemented activities that directly relate to the National Curriculum and 'Literacy Hour' group work. Ideas and activities can also be incorporated into Individual Education Plans.
- Aims to address current concerns about reading standards and to provide support for classroom assistants and parents helping with the teaching of reading.

Class Talk by Rosemary Sage
- Looks at teacher–student communication and reflects on what is happening in the classroom.
- Looks at how students talk in different classroom situations and evaluates this information in terms of planning children's learning.
- Considers the problems of transmitting meaning to others.
- Discusses and reflects on practical strategies to improve the quality of talking, teaching and learning.

OTHER TITLES FROM NEP

Effective Resources for Able and Talented Children by Barry Teare
- A practical sequel to Barry Teare's Effective Provision for Able and Talented Children (see above), which can nevertheless be used entirely independently.
- Contains a wealth of photocopiable resources for able and talented pupils in both the primary and secondary sectors.
- Provides activities designed to inspire, motivate, challenge and stretch able children, encouraging them to enjoy their true potential.
- Resources are organised into National Curriculum areas, such as Literacy, Science and Humanities, each preceded by a commentary outlining key principles and giving general guidance for teachers.

More Effective Resources for Able and Talented Children by Barry Teare
- A treasury of stimulating and challenging activities to provide excitement and enrichment for more able children of all ages.
- can be used in situations both within and beyond normal classroom lessons, including differentiated homework, summer schools, clubs and competitions.
- All activities are photocopiable and accompanied by comprehensive solutions and notes for teachers.
- Resources are divided into several themes: English and literacy; mathematics and numeracy; science; humanities, citizenship, problem solving, decision making and information processing; modern foreign languages; young children; logical thought; detective work and codes; lateral thinking; competitions.

Imagine That... by Stephen Bowkett
- Hands-on, user-friendly manual for stimulating creative thinking, talking and writing in the classroom.
- Provides over 100 practical and immediately useable classroom activities and games that can be used in isolation, or in combination, to help meet the requirements and standards of the National Curriculum.
- Explores the nature of creative thinking and how this can be effectively driven through an ethos of positive encouragement, mutual support and celebration of success and achievement.
- Empowers children to learn how to learn.

Self-Intelligence by Stephen Bowkett
- Helps explore and develop emotional resourcefulness in teachers and their pupils.
- Aims to help teachers and pupils develop the high-esteem that underpins success in education.